THE DECADES OF TWENTIETH-CENTURY AMERICA

AMERICA IN THE 1930s

EDMUND LINDOP with
MARGARET J. GOLDSTEIN

TFCB Twenty-First Century Books · Minneapolis

Twenty-First Century Books
A division of Lerner Publishing Group, Inc.
241 First Avenue North
Minneapolis, MN 55401 U.S.A.

Website address: www.lernerbooks.com

Library of Congress Cataloging-in-Publication Data

Lindop, Edmund.
     America in the 1930s / Edmund Lindop with Margaret J.
Goldstein.
          p.   cm. — (The decades of twentieth-century America)
     Includes bibliographical references and index.
     ISBN 978–0–7613–2832–2 (lib. bdg. : alk. paper)
     1. United States—History—1933–1945—Juvenile literature.
     2. New Deal, 1933–1939—Juvenile literature. 3. Nineteen
     thirties—Juvenile literature. I. Title.
     E809.L565 2010
     973.917—dc22   2007042902

Manufactured in the United States of America
1 2 3 4 5 6 – PA – 15 14 13 12 11 10

CONTENTS ★★★★★★★★★★★★★★★★★★★★★★★★

Ford Motor Company WORKERS ASSEMBLE CARS ON A LINE
at a plant in Dearborn, Michigan, in the 1920s.

CRASH

The year was 1929—the last year of the "Roaring Twenties," as the decade was often called. The nickname was certainly appropriate. In the 1920s, the United States seemed to be roaring full steam ahead.

It was a decade of newness. Cars were a new invention. In 1920 less than one-third of U.S. families owned a car. By 1929 more than 80 percent owned one, and new cars rolled off the assembly line at the rate of one every ten seconds. Radio was a new invention. The first commercial radio show aired in November 1920. By 1929 almost half of all U.S. homes had a cabinet-sized radio in the living room. Motion pictures were a new invention. The first feature-length films—silent films—arrived at movie houses in the late 1910s. By 1929 the films were "talkies" (movies with sound) and Americans were buying 95 million movie tickets each week. Electrical power was a new invention. In 1920 less than half of all urban homes were wired for electricity. By 1930 almost 90 percent of urban dwellers had electricity in their homes. Along with electricity came electrical appliances: washing machines, refrigerators, vacuum cleaners, and irons. All this new technology prompted automaker Henry Ford to exclaim, "Machinery is the new Messiah [God]."

■ "ALL THAT JAZZ"

By 1920 more than half of all Americans lived in towns and cities. With cars, radios, and other new technology, the pace of U.S. life

quickened. The Eighteenth Amendment to the U.S. Constitution (ratified in 1919) made it illegal to manufacture or sell alcohol, but many Americans ignored the law. They drank on the sly, in secret nightclubs called speakeasies. In speakeasies and on the radio, Americans listened to the brand-new sounds of jazz music. Young people did the Charleston and other dances that sent their arms and legs flying. There was an excitement, a buzz in the air.

Women played a big part in this new excitement. In earlier eras, American women had enjoyed few rights and freedoms. They were expected to be modest and to keep their bodies—even their ankles and necks—hidden under layers and layers of clothing. They were expected to stay at home and care for their families. They were certainly not supposed to dance and carouse in speakeasies and jazz clubs.

YOUNG WOMEN DANCE THE CHARLESTON
as part of a dance contest in the 1920s.

But these restrictions began to fall away in the teens and twenties. In 1920 the Nineteenth Amendment to the U.S. Constitution gave American women the right to vote. Around the same time, young women began to wear shorter skirts, revealing their legs from the knees on down. Even more scandalous, some young women smooched with their boyfriends in the backseats of cars. They accompanied men to speakeasies, where they danced, drank, and smoked cigarettes. They enjoyed being wicked and breaking the rules of their old-fashioned parents.

■ BUY NOW, PAY LATER

The United States enjoyed good economic health in the 1920s, but not everyone was rich or even middle class. Farmers struggled from one harvest to the next. Factory workers struggled from one paycheck to the next. Many African Americans were desperately poor. But the nation as a whole prospered. In general, Ameri-cans of the 1920s were wealthier, healthier, better fed, and more comfortable than at any previous time in their history.

Under President Calvin Coolidge, the economy chugged along. Factories churned out cars, appliances, clothing, toiletries, and other consumer goods. At grocery stores, consumers found shelves full of breakfast cereal, soap, and soup—all processed, packaged, and stamped with brand names. Advertising became almost an art form as ad agencies figured out which kinds of slogans and illustrations best persuaded consumers to buy.

And what if a buyer didn't have all the money for that Model T Ford or that Kenmore electric washing machine? Simple: sellers introduced the installment plan. Buyers could get that new Kenmore ($79.50) for just $5 down and $5 a month afterward. Most Americans didn't worry about managing the monthly payments. After all, the economy was strong

Buyers could get that new Kenmore for just $5 down and $5 a month afterward. Most Americans didn't worry about managing the monthly payments.

and industry was booming. Americans had money in their pockets and were eager to spend it on the latest and greatest gadgets.

"PENNIES FROM HEAVEN"

"Everybody was raking in money with a shovel." That's how humorist and newspaper columnist Will Rogers described the U.S. stock market in 1929. Rogers was exaggerating, of course—but not that much. Since 1924 the stock market had been climbing higher by the minute. That meant money—sometimes big money—for those who invested in stocks. In March 1928, one share of Radio Corporation of America (RCA) stock cost $77. That same share was worth more than $400 by the end of the year—a $323 per-share profit for the buyer who bought in March and sold in December.

"Buy now, pay later" applied not only to consumer goods but also to stock purchases. Investors bought "on margin," or credit. They put down a little money, perhaps 10 or 20 percent of the stock price, and borrowed the rest from a broker. If stock prices rose—and buyers were certain that they would—investors could easily pay off their loans with the big profits they netted.

Americans were eager to make a killing in the market. Some invested their life savings in stocks, while others mortgaged (borrowed against the value of) their homes. Many banks invested all the money that depositors had left there for safekeeping.

The get-rich-quick scheme worked—for a while. Investors were making so much money that it was easy to brush aside warnings that the bubble might burst. But, in fact, many stock prices were overvalued. The companies that people invested in weren't necessarily thriving or profitable, and some companies were out-and-out frauds—created only to capture the money of starry-eyed investors.

BLACK TUESDAY

Officials at the Federal Reserve, the government agency that oversees the nation's banking system, saw that the stock market was out of control. To slow the market, the agency raised interest rates in August 1929. Higher interest rates meant that it cost more to borrow money. With less easy money at their fingertips, some investors got nervous. They began to buy fewer stocks. With less demand from buyers, stock prices began to fall.

As the market turned downward, more people worried. What if they lost all their investments and also had to pay back loans to their brokers? More and more people began to sell, and stock prices fell even further. The market sputtered along through September and October, with stock prices falling a little and then recovering.

Then, on October 29, 1929, the bottom dropped out altogether. On that day—Black Tuesday—investors went into a mass panic and sold more than 16 million shares of stock. Almost instantly, once high-flying stocks were practically worthless.

Suddenly, billions of dollars had vanished from the U.S. economy. Ordinary investors lost their homes and life savings. Even some millionaires went bankrupt.

The front page of the *Brooklyn Daily Eagle* screams the fear on Wall Street following the stock market's initial crash on October 24, 1929, known as **BLACK THURSDAY**.

The events of Black Tuesday didn't directly affect most Americans. In fact, only about 2.5 percent of Americans had stock investments in 1929. But the stock market crash did affect the economy as a whole. The crash shook people's confidence in U.S. financial systems. Worried about the economy, people were suddenly afraid to spend money. And when people spent less, businesses suffered.

Banks were some of the biggest losers on Black Tuesday. They had invested their depositors' money, and all of a sudden, that money was gone. Some banks went completely broke. Many Americans no longer trusted banks to keep their money safe. In city after city, depositors rushed to withdraw their savings. They hid their money at home—under floorboards and mattresses—for safekeeping. When people pulled their money out, more banks went out of business. The remaining banks didn't have enough money left to invest in new businesses.

DEPOSITORS CROWD A BANK TO WITHDRAW THEIR MONEY. The bank failures following the stock market crash of 1929 made many Americans afraid to leave their money in banks.

It was a vicious downward spiral. With fewer bank loans and less consumer spending, businesses cut back more and more. They made fewer products. They began to lay off workers. Americans looked around and saw their friends and neighbors losing their jobs. They naturally worried: Is my job safe? Can I afford to pay for my house, my car, and my electric washing machine? Can I afford food for my family? Gripped by fear, people became afraid to spend money and invest in new business ventures—and so the downward spiral continued.

This was the atmosphere in late 1929. The Roaring Twenties were no longer roaring. The nation that had danced and drunk and driven fast cars for ten years was in a tailspin. It had entered a darker era—quickly labeled the Great Depression (1929–1942). As a new decade dawned, a feeling of despair seeped through the American psyche. What would the future bring? People prepared for the worst.

11

This photograph from the 1930s shows MEN STANDING IN LINE AT THE STATE EMPLOYMENT OFFICE in San Francisco, California.

CHAPTER ONE

HARD HIT:
THE GREAT DEPRESSION

In 1931 Ed Paulsen was nineteen years old—young, strong, and eager to work. He and his two brothers had moved to San Francisco, California, from their home in South Dakota. The young men hoped for a bright future in the big city. What they found instead were unemployed men—hordes of them, long lines of them. Some of the men milled around the city's docks, waiting for jobs. Others, having given up on job hunting, lined up at soup kitchens, waiting for something to eat. Paulsen remembered:

> I'd get up at five in the morning and head for the waterfront. Outside the Spreckles Sugar Refinery, outside the gates, there would be a thousand men. You know dang well there's only three or four jobs. The guy [boss] would come out with two little Pinkerton cops [security guards]: "I need two guys [workers]...." A thousand men would fight like a pack of Alaskan dogs to get through there.

After the boss selected just two workers, the crowd dispersed. The men drifted off to city parks and street corners or perhaps to the Salvation Army, which was handing out food.

Most of the job seekers were fathers, Paulsen recalled. They were hungry and desperate.

Paulsen and his brothers stayed hopeful. "You watched the papers, you listened to rumors, you'd get word somebody's gonna build a building," he remembered. "So the next morning you get up at five o'clock and you dash over there. You got a big tip. [But] there's three thousand men there, carpenters, cement men, guys who knew machinery and everything else.... More and more men were after fewer and fewer jobs."

The situation that Paulsen found in San Francisco repeated itself in city after city: New York, Chicago, Pittsburgh, Cleveland. By 1931 the United States was deep into the Great Depression. Millions were unemployed, millions were homeless, and millions were hungry. This was the grim reality facing the nation at the start of the 1930s.

■ A NATION IN CRISIS

On the heels of the 1929 stock market crash, the U.S. economy collapsed. More than twenty-five thousand businesses went broke in 1930. Sales of Model A Fords dropped 50 percent that same year. More than thirteen hundred banks closed in 1930—wiping out billions of dollars in hard-earned savings. "It was a terrible time," remembered one depositor, whose money was all lost when the formerly prosperous United States Bank closed. "You felt as though the bottom had dropped out of your life."

As businesses foundered and failed, they had to cut wages and staff. Unemployment figures nearly tripled—from about 1.5 million unemployed in 1929 to 4.3 million in 1930. By 1933 the number had tripled again: 12.8 million people—almost one-quarter of the U.S. labor force—were unemployed.

■ "BROTHER, CAN YOU SPARE A DIME?"

In the 1930s, men were typically the family breadwinners. Determined to care for their wives and children, men who lost jobs in the early 1930s resolutely set out to find new work. Dressed in shined shoes and their best business clothes, they scoured the want ads, waited in line at employment agencies, and stood outside factories and building sites with thousands of other job seekers. But

no one was hiring new workers—they were laying off old ones instead. Every day, as more businesses shut down, more men joined the job search.

Many men took odd jobs, such as shining shoes or doing chores for neighbors. Some sold the family furniture to raise cash. Thousands took up an offer from the International Apple Shippers' Association. They bought surplus apples on credit and sold them for nickels on city streets. By the end of 1930, six thousand men—some of them former executives—were selling apples in New York City. Any job would do. "I would be only too glad to dig ditches to keep my family from going hungry," wrote a North Carolina man in 1933.

After months of searching, the job seekers' clothes grew shabby. Their shoes wore out. Eventually, hopelessness took over. More and more men simply sat on park benches all day. Some begged, while others stole food from grocery stores. Many turned to drink. Suicide rates rose.

UNEMPLOYED MEN SLEEP IN A PARK in Minneapolis, Minnesota, during the late 1930s.

At night, men returned to their hungry families. They found the bills piled up, the rent overdue, and the gas company threatening to turn off the heat. In Philadelphia, Pennsylvania, families were evicted at the rate of thirteen hundred a month. "No home, no work, no money," a Pennsylvania man lamented in 1934. "We cannot go along this way. They have shut the water supply from us. No means of sanitation. We can not keep the children clean."

Some people moved to cheaper housing—unheated tenements, where many families shared one bathroom. Others moved to the streets, sleeping on benches or under bridges. Those who were lucky might find shelter at night in a city building, a church, or a cheap rooming house.

In Oakland, California, some families made their homes inside big sewer pipes. In Arkansas some people lived in caves. In New York and other cities, shantytowns sprung up in vacant lots. The houses there were crude shacks, cobbled together out of scrap metal, tarpaper, cardboard, and old wooden crates. People sneeringly called these villages Hoovervilles, after U.S. president Herbert Hoover. Many blamed him for the Great Depression.

THIS HOOVERVILLE sprang up outside of Seattle, Washington, during the mid-1930s.

When most people think of President Herbert Hoover, they think of the Great Depression—and Hoover's failure to help the U.S. economy. Hoover earned such a bad reputation in the 1930s that many people forget about his many achievements earlier in the century.

Herbert Hoover was born in Iowa in 1874. He graduated from Stanford University with a degree in engineering. He worked as a mining engineer in California, Australia, and China. In 1908 he founded his own engineering firm, which did business all around the world.

Hoover got involved with government during World War I (1914–1918). While on business in London, England, he organized a committee to supply food to war-torn Belgium. The United States entered the war in 1917, and Hoover became head of the U.S. Food Administration. This government agency oversaw the pricing, production, and distribution of food during wartime.

After the war, Hoover headed the American Relief Administration, which shipped food to millions of needy Europeans. He also organized aid for starving Russians after their country was torn apart by revolution and civil war. Hoover's next position was secretary of commerce under President Warren G. Harding. He kept the job during the Calvin Coolidge administration.

In 1928 the Republicans nominated Hoover as their presidential candidate. "We in America today are nearer to the

HERBERT HOOVER became president of the United States in 1929, right before the nation entered the Great Depression.

final triumph over poverty than ever before in the history of any land," he said when accepting the nomination. Hoover beat the Democratic candidate, Alfred E. Smith, in a landslide.

Despite Hoover's optimistic words, the stock market crashed and poverty triumphed. As the Depression deepened, Americans dragged Hoover's name through the mud. They called homeless encampments Hoovervilles. They turned empty pockets inside out and called them Hoover flags. When Hoover ran for president again in 1932, against Democrat Franklin Roosevelt, he found few supporters.

Badly beaten in the election, Hoover retired from politics. He traveled, lectured, wrote books, and worked with educational and charitable groups. In the late 1940s and early 1950s, he advised the administrations of U.S. presidents Harry S. Truman and Dwight D. Eisenhower. Hoover died in 1964.

Herbert Hoover tried several tactics to fight the nation's economic free fall. He thought that increasing tariffs might help. These taxes on imported goods were designed to make foreign products more expensive and to encourage people to buy cheaper products made at home. In 1930 U.S. tariffs were already high, but President Hoover wanted to make them higher. If people bought fewer foreign goods and more U.S. ones, he reasoned, the U.S. economy would benefit. With Hoover's backing, Congress passed the Smoot-Hawley Tariff Act of 1930.

Hoover's plan did not work. Higher tariffs hurt foreign businesses, since it became harder for them to sell goods in the United States. As business slowed, foreign economies also began to suffer. Tightening their belts, foreign companies bought fewer products from the United States. The U.S. tariffs and other economic policies fed into another vicious cycle, with people buying less and companies laying off workers— only the problem had become global. The Depression engulfed the whole world.

The stories of the Depression in foreign countries are just as wrenching as those from the United States. From Great Britain to Brazil to Australia, people faced unemployment, hunger, and homelessness. One British man walked the streets of London with a sign on his back. It read: "I know 3 trades, I speak 3 languages, fought for 3 years, have 3 children, and no work for 3 months, but I only want one job."

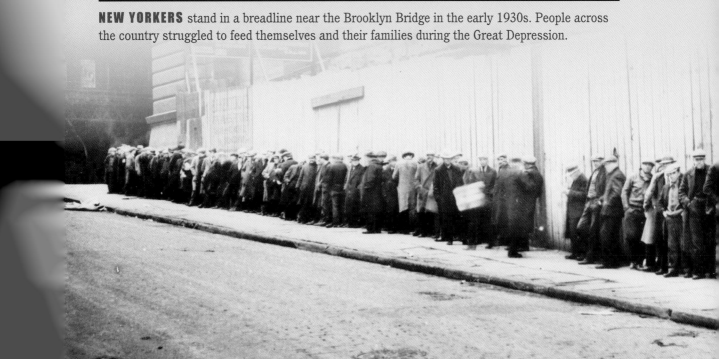

NEW YORKERS stand in a breadline near the Brooklyn Bridge in the early 1930s. People across the country struggled to feed themselves and their families during the Great Depression.

Hunger went hand in hand with homelessness. In rural areas, people made meals out of berries and edible weeds. Some hunted rabbits and other small animals. In big cities, people rummaged through garbage cans looking for scraps of food. Some literally starved to death. Charities set up soup kitchens to feed the hungry. In New York in 1931, eighty-two soup kitchens served an estimated eighty-five thousand meals a day. Shivering and starving, people stood in line for hours waiting for a slice of bread and a bowl of thin soup.

■ RAMBLIN' ROUND

Desperate and despondent, vast numbers of men left home. From small towns in the Midwest, they headed to Chicago or Detroit, hoping to find jobs in the big city. Others didn't necessarily have a destination. They just imagined that things *had* to be better someplace else. So they walked, hitchhiked, and sneaked into railroad cars, bound for who knows where.

By the hundreds of thousands, men became hoboes. They crisscrossed the country, looking for jobs that

didn't exist. In towns along the way, the travelers asked for odd jobs and handouts. More often than not, the local sheriff chased them out of town or threw them in jail for vagrancy. Security guards rousted them off trains and out of rail yards.

Folksinger Woody Guthrie joined the hobo army in 1937. Lured by the promise of good-paying jobs in California, he hitchhiked and rode freight trains west out of Texas. In Tucson, Arizona, broke and weak from hunger, Guthrie knocked on a stranger's door. "I'm wondering if you've got a job of work that I could do to earn a bite to eat, little snack of some kind. Grass cut. Scrape leaves. Trim some hedge. Anything like that," he inquired. The householder, a minister's wife, whispered back through the screen door, "Listen young man . . . there's a dozen of you people that come around here every day knocking on this door. . . . If the minister starts out to feed one of you, you'll go off and tell a dozen others about it, and then they'll all be down here wanting something to eat."

Guthrie was one of the lucky ones. He made it safely to California and eventually earned money playing music. Others found only despair along the nation's roads and railroads. Camped out amid piles of tin cans and broken bottles, the hoboes were "a pitiful sight," wrote Tom Kromer in his 1935 novel *Waiting for Nothing*. "These stiffs with their ragged clothes and their sunken cheeks. . . . They huddle around their fires in the night. Tomorrow they will huddle around their fires, and the next night, and the next."

In towns along the way, the travelers asked for odd jobs and handouts. More often than not, the local sheriff chased them out of town.

◼ HALF RATIONS

Not everyone was unemployed, of course, but just having a job did not guarantee a full stomach in the 1930s. Many employers kept their businesses open during the Depression by cutting workers' hours or wages. Rubber manufacturers cut the workweek from forty hours to thirty, resulting in a 25 percent pay cut for workers. Henry Ford, who once paid his factory workers between five and seven dollars a day, cut wages to four dollars per day in 1932 and speeded up his assembly lines.

More than two million men served in the U.S. military during World War I. This fighting unit was called the American Expeditionary Force, and it helped the United States and its allies win the war. In 1924 a grateful Congress voted to give World War I veterans a bonus: $1.25 for each day of overseas military service and $1 for each day served in the United States—but the bonus wouldn't be paid until 1945.

By 1932 many World War I veterans were homeless and hungry. To help the veterans, Congressman Wright Patman of Texas introduced a bill that would make the bonus payable at once. For most veterans, the payment would have amounted to a few hundred dollars—which would have been a lifesaver in 1932.

Walter Waters, an unemployed cannery worker and a World War I vet, thought that the presence of veterans in Washington, D.C., might influence Congress to support the Patman Bill. Waters left Portland, Oregon, in May, traveling to Washington by boxcar. Word spread, and other veterans joined Patman. Eventually, about fifteen thousand veterans, some with their families, poured into the nation's capital.

Calling themselves the Bonus Expeditionary Force, or Bonus Army, the veterans settled down, some in abandoned government buildings but most in ramshackle camps. The largest camp was along the Anacostia River.

Despite pressure from the veterans, on June 17, 1932, the Senate defeated the Patman Bill. But most of the Bonus Army stayed on, vowing to get their bonuses. The following month, the Washington police tried to oust the veterans. During a scuffle, the police killed two men. After that, President Hoover called in the armed forces to evict the protesters.

Under the command of General Douglas MacArthur, cavalry, infantry, and tanks moved in to clear out the Anacostia encampment. The infantry attacked with tear gas and bayonets. One baby died from the gas, and several veterans were wounded. As night fell, the Bonus Army's shantytown went up in flames. The survivors straggled out of Washington.

The sight of U.S. soldiers attacking peaceful marchers alarmed Americans. Many already disliked Herbert Hoover. The attack on the Bonus Army earned him even more critics.

Police remove BONUS ARMY MARCHERS from their camp outside Washington, D.C., in 1932.

21

Instead of 232 cars a day, workers had to build 535 cars. The pace was exhausting—and the paycheck was smaller—but most Ford employees were happy to have a job at all. By then the Ford Motor Company had already closed many of its plants and fired tens of thousands of workers.

People lived on a shoestring. They skimped, scrounged, and skipped meals. Some borrowed money, while others moved in with friends or family. To cut down on grocery purchases, women planted backyard gardens and

U.S. farms had boomed during World War I, when the warring nations of Europe were desperate for wheat and other food crops. To meet the demand, farmers on the Great Plains plowed more and more land and bought bigger and better equipment. Many borrowed money to expand their farms.

But once the war ended, demand fell and so did prices. U.S. farmers struggled through the 1920s. Prices of wheat and hogs, which had once been huge moneymakers, fell steadily. As farm income slid downward

People lived on a shoestring. They skimped, scrounged, and skipped meals. Some borrowed money, while others moved in with friends or family.

canned their own vegetables. Some people made clothes out of scrap cloth, and almost everyone mended old clothes. To help with the family bills, children took after-school jobs: mowing lawns, babysitting, and shoveling snow. With families scrambling for just the basics, luxuries—new cars and new appliances—were out of the question.

■ BOOM AND BUST

The Depression hit farm country earlier and harder than it hit the cities.

in the 1920s, so did the fortunes of banks, suppliers, and other businesses that worked with farms.

By the time the stock market crashed, U.S. farmers were already poor. Then the Depression drove a stake into the heart of farm country. Prices plummeted to all-time lows. A bushel of wheat, which had netted $2.16 after World War I, sold for only 38 cents by 1932. Hogs had sold for $22.18 a piece in 1919, but by 1932, the price was $6.31. The price of

farmland fell—from an average of $69 an acre (0.4 hectares) in 1920 to just $30 an acre (0.4 hectares) by the end of 1932.

All across rural America, people despaired. "We can't make the winter [we] are all bare foot," mourned one mother. "The 13 years boy and the 7 years old is just naked, no shoes, nor clothes. We lost all we had three years ago and have made crop failure ever since. . . . I can't see how we will get by."

Most farmers owed money to bankers. If a farmer couldn't pay the loan, the bank foreclosed on the property. The bank held an auction, selling the land, livestock, and equipment to the highest bidders. The farmer—and any tenants who rented land from the farmer—had to leave.

Sometimes, farmers resorted to drastic measures to save their neighbors from foreclosure. In Le Mars, Iowa, an angry mob threatened to string up the local judge who was ordering farm foreclosures. Farmers sometimes packed into auctions and threatened anyone who made a realistic bid. Instead, as each

23

Military police supervise **A FARM AUCTION IN IOWA** in the 1930s to keep farmers from disrupting the sale.

animal or piece of equipment came up for sale, the farmers made superlow bids, such as thirty-five cents for a cow. When the auction was over, the buyers gave all their low-priced purchases, including the land, back to the farmer in foreclosure.

Although successful in a few cases, such tactics couldn't stem the tide of foreclosures. While big businesses kept farming large stretches of land, most single-family farmers went broke. They and their tenants packed up what little they had left. By the thousands, they joined the ranks of the unemployed, the underfed, and the hoboes riding the rails.

■ DUST BOWL DISASTER

It seemed as if things couldn't get worse for the U.S. farmer, but they did—much worse. Drought hit the Great Plains in 1931. Rain didn't fall and the soil dried up, making it harder and harder to scratch a living from the land. Then, two years later, fierce windstorms began to blow across the Great Plains.

In the 1910s and 1920s, farmers had expanded their acreage by planting previously untouched prairie. They had plowed the native grasses that held the topsoil in place. When the windstorms hit in 1933, the soil was not only dry but also loose. It blew away in vast clouds of dust. For the next five years, a series of dust storms swept across North and South Dakota, Nebraska, Kansas, Oklahoma, Texas, and surrounding farm states—an area soon nicknamed the dust bowl.

With winds up to 70 miles (113 kilometers) per hour, the storms buried crops and farm machinery under knee-deep piles of dust. The dust shut down highways and killed livestock. In the spring of 1935, one storm destroyed half the wheat crop in Kansas and all the wheat in Nebraska. The storms came in waves—sometimes more than one a day and sometimes for weeks on end. When a dust storm hit, the sky grew black. "This is the ultimate darkness," wrote one Kansan about the "black blizzard" of April 1935. "So must come the end of the world."

The storms came in waves—sometimes more than one a day and sometimes for weeks on end. When a dust storm hit, the sky grew black.

WINDSTORMS BLEW TONS OF DUST ACROSS THE GREAT PLAINS. It piled up against buildings like this one in Oklahoma.

The finely ground dust was relentless. It blew into houses, covering furniture, floors, and walls. People protected their noses and mouths with handkerchiefs, but they still swallowed and breathed in dust. Dust clotted their hair and stung their eyes. "Our faces were as dirty as if we had rolled in the dirt," remembered one dust bowl resident. "Our hair was gray and stiff and we ground dirt between our teeth."

Householders plugged the cracks around their doors and windows with wet rags, but still the dust got inside. It got into food and water and wrecked havoc on the lungs. People grew sick with raw throats, coughing, chest pains, and shortness of breath. The "dust pneumonia," as doctors labeled an array of respiratory illnesses, sickened thousands and killed hundreds.

■ GONE WEST

Beset by hunger, dust, and desperation, the dust bowl farmers began a great migration west. They packed up what little they owned and headed for California by car. Word was that the big fruit farms there needed workers. Family after family set out with furniture, bedding, pots, and skillets strapped to the tops of their jalopies (rickety cars and trucks). The migrants rumbled west along Route 66, certain that jobs awaited them in California. By 1938 more than two hundred thousand had hit the road.

But the refugees were in for a rude awakening. Just getting to California was treacherous. The old cars broke down and ran out of gas. The destitute

DUST BOWL FAMILIES WHO MADE IT TO CALIFORNIA often lived in tent camps and shacks.

migrants ran out of food and money. They camped on the side of the road, broke and hungry. In cities along the way, people sneered at their ragged caravans, and sheriffs hustled them out of town.

Once they reached California, the abuse grew fiercer. The newcomers were "shiftless trash who live like hogs," remarked one California doctor. Californians labeled the migrants Okies, for "Oklahoma," no matter whether they came from Oklahoma, Kansas, or another dust bowl state. Police turned many of them back at the state line.

California needed fruit pickers—it was true—but there wasn't nearly enough work for the thousands upon thousands of refugees who streamed in from the Great Plains. With so many desperate for work, farm owners could pay laborers next to nothing.

In 1939 writer John Steinbeck vividly portrayed the plight of dust bowl refugees in his monumental novel *The Grapes of Wrath.* Having fled the Oklahoma drought, Steinbeck's Joad family learns the harsh reality of the California labor market, where labor contractors prey on people who are "so goddamn hungry they'll work for nothin' but biscuits."

Although fiction, Steinbeck's book accurately showed the reality for dust bowl migrants. For them and millions of other Americans, it appeared that the numbers were stacked against them, that the system was stacked against them. Almost everyone agreed: the system needed changing.

Outgoing president HERBERT HOOVER *(left)* and president-elect FRANKLIN ROOSEVELT
ride through Washington, D.C., to Roosevelt's inauguration in 1933.

CHAPTER TWO

A NEW DEAL:
GOVERNMENT FIGHTS THE GREAT DEPRESSION

No one knew how long the Depression would last, but President Hoover was optimistic about economic recovery. On May 1, 1930, he told a gathering of the U.S. Chamber of Commerce, "We have been passing through one of those great economic storms which periodically bring hardship and suffering to our people. While the stock exchange crash occurred only six months ago, I am convinced we have now passed the worst and with continued unity of effort we shall rapidly recover."

Hoover was certain that U.S. businesses would bounce back. He urged big business owners not to cut wages—thus keeping spending money in the pockets of their workers. He urged ordinary Americans to support businesses by spending rather than saving. He also backed passage of the Smoot-Hartley Tariff Act, which cut down on foreign imports and steered people toward U.S.-made products.

One thing Hoover bristled at, however, was the federal government giving handouts to needy people. He thought that federal assistance would undermine Americans' self-reliance. Traditionally, needy Americans had turned for help to family, private charities, and local and state government—not the federal government. Hoover thought this was the best system for handling the current crisis.

While refusing to supply direct relief for individuals, Hoover did assist businesses. His main program was the Reconstruction Finance Corporation (RFC). Created in January 1932, the RFC lent money to banks and other businesses so that they could open new facilities and hire more workers.

Despite Hoover's best efforts, unemployment figures kept rising, and income kept falling. Banks and businesses kept going broke. Eventually, Hoover did authorize some federal relief programs for needy citizens—but it was too little too late. By the end of 1932, three years into the Great Depression, Americans were desperate for help—and hungry for a change of leadership.

■ FDR

It was time for a presidential election. The Republicans, not wanting to acknowledge that their old policies had failed, again nominated Herbert Hoover. Privately, most Republicans admitted that they were unlikely to win the election—no matter whom they nominated. By 1932 many working-class Americans despised the Republican Party as much as they despised Herbert Hoover. It was the party of big business and big bankers. It was the party that had carried the nation into the Depression and failed to reduce people's suffering.

The Democrats seemed certain to win the White House. They nominated Franklin D. Roosevelt, the charismatic and liberal governor of New York. Roosevelt had a kind of magic about him. He was witty and handsome and flashed a bright smile. He came from a wealthy family, yet he seemed to understand the common people.

Presidential candidate **FRANKLIN D. ROOSEVELT** *(far right)* talks to farmers in Georgia on the campaign trail in 1932.

Franklin D. Roosevelt (often called by his initials, FDR) was born in Hyde Park, New York, in 1882. His father, James Roosevelt, had made a fortune in the railroad and shipping industries. Young Franklin enjoyed a privileged childhood. He attended the Groton School, a private boarding school in Massachusetts.

Roosevelt entered Harvard University in 1900 and Columbia University Law School in 1904. One year later, he married Eleanor Roosevelt, his fifth cousin and a niece of President Theodore Roosevelt. The couple eventually had six children, one of whom died in infancy.

In 1907 Roosevelt began work with a New York City law firm. In the fall of 1910, he entered politics, running for a seat in the New York State Senate. Charming on the campaign trail, Roosevelt won the election and held the job for two terms.

President Woodrow Wilson appointed Roosevelt assistant secretary of the U.S. Navy in 1913. Certain that the United States would enter World War I, which it did in 1917, Roosevelt convinced Wilson to provide more ships and sailors for the navy.

In 1920 Roosevelt was the Democratic candidate for vice president. He and his running mate, James Cox, lost the election, and FDR returned to work at his law firm.

In 1921 Roosevelt contracted polio, a disease that partially paralyzed him. For the remainder of his life, he wore braces on

FRANKLIN ROOSEVELT vowed to lead the nation out of the Depression.

his legs and sometimes used crutches and a wheelchair. The illness did not damage his political career, especially since Roosevelt kept his disability hidden from the U.S. public. He stood behind podiums when he spoke and asked photographers not to take pictures that revealed his disability.

FDR became governor of New York State in 1928. His administration spearheaded much progressive legislation, including a farm relief program, pensions for the elderly, and laws to protect workers. FDR won a second term as governor in 1930.

He continued his winning ways in the presidential elections of 1932, 1936, 1940, and 1944. Roosevelt steered the United States through the dark days of the Depression and the equally dark days of World War II (1939–1945). Roosevelt died in April 1945. He remains one of the most beloved presidents in U.S. history.

On the radio, at campaign speeches, and in the newspapers, Roosevelt projected an image of strength and compassion. Few voters knew that he was crippled from polio and that he often used a wheelchair or walked with crutches.

When he accepted the Democratic nomination, Roosevelt promised the nation a "new deal." His campaign song was "Happy Days Are Here Again." Many Americans believed the hype. Some even saw Roosevelt as a saint or savior who would rescue them from their woes.

When Election Day rolled around, Roosevelt racked up a landslide victory. He won almost 23 million votes, compared to 16 million for Hoover, and 472 electoral votes against Hoover's 59. At his inauguration, on March 4, 1933, Roosevelt projected calm and confidence. He told the nation: "The only thing we have to fear is fear itself."

■ "WE DO OUR PART"

Picking up the term he had introduced earlier, Roosevelt immediately launched his New Deal, a program to fix the U.S. economy. First, on March 6, Roosevelt declared a "bank holiday," a shutdown of the nation's banks, designed to prevent further bank failures. All major banks had to close their doors for a few days while government inspectors checked the financial records of each. If a bank was financially sound, it could reopen. The inspectors allowed about half the nation's banks to reopen, but they had to follow new rules that would keep them on firm footing. To protect depositors even more, the government created the Federal Deposit Insurance Corporation (FDIC), which insured people's bank deposits, repaying them if their banks went broke.

Next, Roosevelt moved to help farmers. Farm prices had dropped to new lows, in part because too many crops were flooding the market. Roosevelt and his advisers wanted to reduce the huge surpluses. Congress passed the Agricultural Adjustment Act (AAA) on May 12, 1933. Under this law, the government paid farmers to reduce production—that is, to plow fewer acres and raise fewer animals.

The new law took effect late in the season, after farmers had already planted their crops and birthed livestock. To get their AAA payments,

cotton growers had to "plow under," or destroy, about 30 percent of their crop. Hog producers had to slaughter six million baby pigs instead of raising them for market.

Many Americans were upset that the government was destroying food when people were starving. "How the pigs would help us," wrote a man from Indiana, "if we could only get them to feed and kill, if only two-thirds of the people who are without meat could get [some] this winter and the coming summer. . . . I am only asking our leader to consider sparing the flesh and food that nature has given us."

Making matters worse, when farm owners took land out of production, they also laid off many tenant farmers who worked for them, creating even more unemployment. In the end, the AAA raised farm prices somewhat but not significantly. Even many diehard Roosevelt fans were disappointed with AAA policies.

After the AAA, the next big law out of Congress was the National Industrial Recovery Act, which created the National Recovery Administration (NRA). The NRA set rules and standards for fair business practices. These rules included minimum wages for workers, maximum work hours per week, and the right of workers to join labor unions. The NRA also set rules about pricing and fair competition among businesses. Businesses were not required to join the NRA, but millions did. Member businesses displayed the NRA emblem—the Blue Eagle—and its slogan, "We Do Our Part."

Several New Deal programs created much-needed jobs. The Civilian Conservation Corps (CCC), for instance, employed needy young men ages seventeen to twenty-five.

Postmaster J. J. Kiely displays
NATIONAL RECOVERY ACT SIGNS,
which bear the Blue Eagle.

President Franklin D. Roosevelt sits at his desk to give **A FIRESIDE CHAT** to radio listeners in 1935.

Franklin Roosevelt was a skilled politician. He used charm, diplomacy, and a flair for language to win voters and supporters. He also used the new technology of his era—radio. Although previous presidents had also spoken on radio, Roosevelt used radio skillfully to drum up support for his New Deal programs. On March 12, 1933, less than one week after his inauguration, he gave the first of his famous "Fireside Chats." In a thirteen-minute radio address, he explained the banking crisis to listeners at home. He chose his words carefully, trying to calm Americans—many of whom were near panic that their banks had gone or might go broke. Roosevelt ended his speech with the reassuring words, "[The banking crisis] is your problem no less than it is mine. Together we cannot fail." Even the name of the address was well chosen. "Fireside Chat" conveyed a feeling of warmth, intimacy, and honesty and the idea that Roosevelt was a trusted family member whom Americans welcomed, via their radios, into their living rooms.

After the first Fireside Chat, Roosevelt continued the tradition throughout his twelve-year presidency. In the 1930s, he spoke about New Deal programs, drought on the Great Plains, unemployment, and other pressing topics. In the 1940s, Roosevelt gave stirring speeches concerning World War II. In total, he gave thirty Fireside Chats. Historians estimate that as many as sixty million Americans tuned in for each one. The broadcasts gave people a feeling of personal connection to the president and offered them hope in hard times.

They went to work planting trees, building trails and buildings, fighting forest fires, and doing other work on public lands and in national parks. They lived in camps run by the U.S. Army. The pay was thirty dollars a month (twenty-five dollars of which was sent home to workers' families), plus food, housing, and medical care. A man named Blackie Gold remembered his stint in the CCC. "I really enjoyed it," he recalled. "I had three wonderful square meals a day. No matter what they put on the table, we ate and were glad to get it." Over the course of its nine-year life span, the CCC provided jobs for more than two million men. About 7 percent of the CCC workers were African Americans, who lived and worked in segregated camps and took their orders from white supervisors.

The Public Works Administration (PWA) and Civil Works Administration (CWA) were other jobs programs. The PWA and CWA hired workers to build schools, courthouses, bridges, dams, water systems, roads, hospitals, and other public infrastructure. The pay was low, and hours were limited, but for hungry families, a low-paying, part-time job was much better than no job at all.

The first New Deal programs—the AAA, CCC, NRA, and others—came out of a special three-month session of Congress (March 9 to June 16, 1933) called the Hundred Days. After the Hundred Days, Roosevelt and his advisers continued to create New Deal agencies. Some helped homeowners, tenant farmers, or migrant workers. Others provided jobs, gave food to the needy, or set new regulations for business and the stock market. Commentators called the various New Deal agencies an "alphabet soup," since they were known by their initials: CWA, FERA, FSA, HOLC, NLRA, NYA, REA, and SEC, to name just a handful.

One of the most important of the later New Deal programs was the Works

"Together we cannot fail."

—Franklin Roosevelt, Fireside Chat, March 12, 1933

Progress Administration (later called the Works Projects Administration), or WPA. The WPA was similar to the PWA in that it put people to work building highways, parks, airports, bridges, and other infrastructure.

WPA CONSTRUCTION WORKERS build a road in Pennsylvania in 1936. The WPA gave work to more than three million Americans. Many millions more remained jobless.

The WPA even hired actors, musicians, artists, and writers to make creative works. At its height, the WPA employed more than three million Americans. Social Security—which makes regular payments to the elderly, disabled, and other needy Americans—also had its birth in the post–Hundred Days period.

■ FOR AND AGAINST

Most Americans who benefited from New Deal programs were extremely grateful. Even those who didn't get government jobs or relief payments—and the vast majority didn't—praised the New Deal. Across the nation, love for President Roosevelt reached new levels. Journalist Martha Gellhorn, who worked for the Federal Emergency Relief Association, reported:

> Every house I visited—mill worker or unemployed—had a picture of the President. These ranged from newspaper clippings (in destitute homes) to large [colored] prints, framed in gilt cardboard. The portrait holds the place of honor over the mantel. . . . And the feeling of these people for the President is one of the most remarkable emotional phenomena I have ever met. He is at once God and their

intimate friend; he knows them all by name, knows their little town
and mill, their little lives and problems. And, though everything fails,
he is there, and will not let them down.

In 1936 Roosevelt ran for president again and won in another landslide,
with 61 percent of the popular vote.

Despite his popularity, the president had many critics. His opponents denounced the New Deal programs as Socialism or Communism, systems in
which the government strictly controls business and the economy. Some critics even likened the Roosevelt administration to the Soviet Union, which had
set up a Communist government in 1917.

Critics also charged that New Deal programs coddled the poor—encourag-
ing them to go on government relief instead of fending for themselves. Some
people who didn't need government help said that relief recipients were ir-
responsible and lazy. They complained about paying taxes to help support
"spongers," "chiselers," and "cheats." Additionally, critics balked at the massive cost of the New Deal. To fund the programs, the government borrowed
money. Between 1933 and 1939, the national debt ballooned from $22.5 billion
to $40.5 billion.

Ultimately, the Supreme Court ruled that several New Deal laws, including
the AAA and the NRA, were unconstitutional. But most programs remained in
operation throughout the 1930s.

WORKERS STRIKE at a Chevrolet plant in Flint, Michigan, in 1937. Throughout the 1930s, workers increasingly banded together in labor unions to fight for better working conditions.

CHAPTER THREE

BANNERS AND BANDWAGONS:

POPULAR MOVEMENTS OF THE 1930s

The New Deal had limited success. The AAA did manage to raise farm prices somewhat, the FDIC stabilized the nation's banking system, and other programs were lifesavers for the unemployed. But even the WPA, the largest New Deal jobs program, employed only 3.3 million Americans at any given time, only one-quarter to one-third of those who were out of work. Despite the massive New Deal, the U.S. economy remained bogged down in a depression throughout the 1930s.

With suffering widespread, it's no wonder that many Americans latched onto new ideas, schemes, and philosophies in the 1930s. Ideas ranged from opening cooperative (customer-owned) grocery stores to all-out revolution.

■ COME AND JOIN THE UNION

The typical workingman of the 1930s was lucky to have a job—even if the pay was low, the hours were long, and the work was dangerous. But workers felt angry and frustrated. Why should they toil—often for ten or twelve hours a day and often for starvation wages—while business owners grew rich from their labor? Increasingly in the 1930s, workers joined together into labor unions.

During the probusiness presidencies of the 1920s, unions had been kept very weak. But as the Depression grew worse, workers became more organized. Unlike their predecessors, both President Roosevelt and Labor

Secretary Frances Perkins (the first woman to serve in a Cabinet position) were pro-union. Their New Deal legislation helped strengthen the union movement.

Throughout the 1930s, workers as diverse as longshoremen, pea pickers, coal miners, and journalists joined trade-specific unions. To pressure their bosses, they went on strike, refusing to work until employers met their demands for higher wages or better working conditions. Outside factories and other workplaces, striking workers and their supporters marched with signs, sang songs, chanted, and blocked business entrances—keeping strikebreakers (replacement workers), customers, and others from going inside.

A particularly effective tactic was the sit-down strike, during which workers took over their factories and refused to work or leave. Because the strikers occupied the workplace, strikebreakers couldn't come in to run the machines in their place. In 1937 workers in Flint, Michigan, called a sit-down strike against General Motors. The strike spread to six states and shut down GM plants for forty days. Of the more than forty-seven hundred strikes in 1937, about 10 percent were sit-down strikes.

WOMEN HOLD A SIT-DOWN STRIKE AT A DETROIT WOOLWORTH STORE IN 1937.
The women were fighting for a pay increase and a forty-hour workweek.

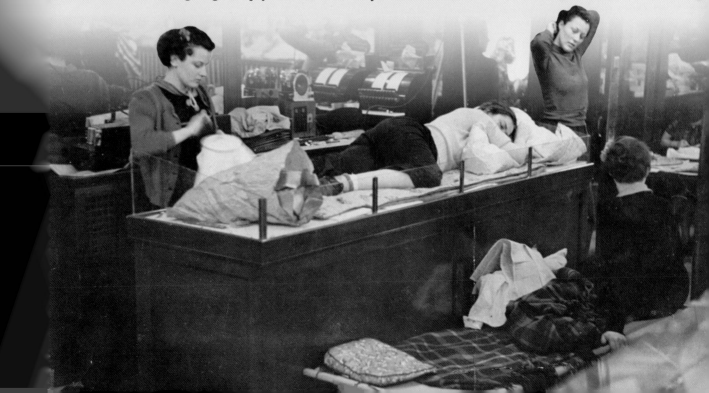

Strikes and union meetings could be boisterous and emotional events. Workers sang "Solidarity Forever," "Hold the Fort," and other songs that encouraged them to stick together and stand up to the bosses. At the General Motors sit-down strike, a worker's wife shouted into a microphone, "Women of Flint, this is your fight! Join the picket line and defend your jobs, your husbands' jobs, and your children's homes."

Unionizing and striking could also be a bloody business. Employers sometimes fired workers who tried to organize unions or had them arrested. Employers sent spies to infiltrate and report on union meetings and had security guards beat striking workers. Many times, strikes turned violent, as strikers, strikebreakers, and police battled it out with clubs, rocks, bottles, and even guns.

Gordon Baxter worked as an attorney for a large auto parts manufacturer in Chicago, Illinois, in the 1930s. He remembers a Chicago police detail called the Industrial Squad. During strikes, "They'd beat them [the strikers] up, put them in jail, make it pretty clear to them to get the hell out of town."

Union organizers got similar treatment. "Uniformed men would come in and arrest the organizer, beat hell out of him, put him in jail," Baxter recalls." Employers kept lists of "agitators" and "troublemakers" who tried to organize unions, and they shared these "black-lists" with one another. Employers wouldn't hire workers whose names appeared on the lists.

Often employers whipped up public hatred toward strikers by calling them Communists or "reds" (the color

> **"Women of Flint, this is your fight! Join the picket line and defend your jobs, your husbands' jobs, and your children's homes."**

—*wife of striking General Motors worker, 1937*

associated with the revolutionaries in the Soviet Union). In fact, some union organizers were Socialists or Communists. But most rank-and-file union members were more politically mainstream. They had no interest in changing the U.S. economy. They joined unions and took part in strikes only because they wanted a fair wage and decent working conditions.

LAW OFFICERS BATTLE WITH STRIKERS outside of a factory in Pennsylvania in 1933.

Strikes certainly hurt employers—keeping them from doing business as long as a strike went on. But many times, employers simply outlasted workers. Striking workers received no paychecks. What little money they got during a strike came from union strike funds. Often strikers eventually gave in and returned to work because they needed income.

■ LEADERS AND FOLLOWERS

The U.S. government created dozens of New Deal programs. Workers organized, struck, and won concessions from their bosses—but still the Depression wore on. How it would end was anyone's guess, but almost everyone, it seemed, had an opinion. Hoboes riding the rails talked politics and economics until late into the night. The Communist Party USA (CPUSA) tried to convince Americans that Communism would solve the nation's problems. CPUSA organizers signed up thousands of new members at Hoovervilles, unemployment offices, and union meetings. On college campuses, students talked politics endlessly and flocked to meetings of the Young People's Socialist League, the Young Communist International, and the Student League for Industrial Democracy.

> **" [Steinbeck] comes right out in plain old English and says . . . you got to . . . stick together . . . till you get [your] job, and get your farm back, and your house and your chickens and your groceries and your clothes, and your money back."**

—Woody Guthrie, in one of his **Woody Sez** *columns, which ran in 1939 and 1940 in* **People's World,** *commenting on* **The Grapes of Wrath,** *the film based on John Steinbeck's 1939 novel*

Economic schemes abounded. One of them came from Francis Townsend, a California doctor. His idea, called the Old-Age Revolving Pension Plan, was designed to help the nation's elderly people—one of the groups hit hardest by the Depression—and boost the economy all at the same time. Townsend proposed that Americans pay a 2 percent sales tax on all purchases. That money would go to pay a pension of two hundred dollars a month to each American aged sixty or older. The pensioners would be required to spend all the money each month, thereby infusing cash into the U.S. economy. The plan was appealing, and "Townsend Clubs" formed all across the nation, with millions attending meetings and signing petitions in support of Townsend's ideas. Economists, however, pointed out that Townsend's plan would place an enormous burden on taxpayers, create higher prices, and cost a fortune to administer. Despite its popular following, government and business dismissed the plan as foolhardy.

Writer and politician Upton Sinclair had a different plan for the economy. Sinclair had come to fame earlier in the century with publication of *The Jungle* (1906). This novel had exposed unsanitary conditions in the nation's meat-packing industry and had led to the passage of food safety laws. In 1933 Sinclair announced that he was running for governor of California on the Democratic ticket. He outlined a program called EPIC, which stood for End Poverty in California. The plan

NOVELIST UPTON SINCLAIR discusses his plan to end poverty in California in a radio speech in 1934.

involved a network of nonprofit, state-run businesses; "land colonies" where workers would grow their own food; cooperative stores; and other economic reforms. Like Francis Townsend, Upton Sinclair attracted many followers from the working class. But to other Americans, his ideas sounded like Socialism—and indeed Sinclair had been a Socialist before switching to the Democratic Party to run for governor. California's business community was alarmed and launched an all-out attack against Sinclair. Using newspaper editorials, radio ads, billboards, and staged newsreels, the anti-Sinclair forces smeared him and assured a victory for his Republican opponent.

More famous than Townsend or Sinclair was Huey Long, a popular (and corrupt) Louisiana governor and then senator. Long's scheme to fight the Depression was called Share Our Wealth. Its motto was "Every Man a King."

LOUISIANA POLITICIAN HUEY LONG *(seated at right)* speaks with journalists about his presidential candidacy in 1935.

	1930s	2000s (first decade)
Average U.S. worker's income	$1,200	$35,000

TYPICAL PRICES

	1930s	2000s (first decade)
Candy bar	5¢	75¢
Bottle of soda	5¢	$1.00
Loaf of bread	8¢	$2.79
Quart of milk	10¢	$1.79
Movie ticket	20¢	$9.00
Man's haircut	25¢	$30.00
Pair of men's shoes	$2.48	$79.99
Child's bicycle	$29.95	$139.99
Washing machine	$47.50	$809.99
Two-door car	$795	$20,000
Three-bedroom house	$5,000	$300,000

(Prices are samples only. At any given time, prices vary by year, location, size, brand, and model.)

Long proposed using the U.S. tax system to redistribute the nation's wealth—ensuring that no one grew too rich and no one remained too poor. No stranger to colorful language, Long called the wealthiest Americans "pigs swilling in the trough of luxury."

In 1934 the Share Our Wealth movement caught fire in the South and quickly spread across the nation. Long decided to run for president in 1936, an idea that terrified the Roosevelt administration. They worried not so much that Long would win the election but that he would split the Democratic vote, thereby handing victory to the Republicans. Long's presidential aspirations died along with Long himself, who fell to an assassin's bullet on September 8, 1935. With its leader gone, the Share Our Wealth movement soon disbanded.

Fighting poverty, homelessness, and injustice in the 1930s seemed like an uphill battle. For Dorothy Day, it was a battle that had to be fought. Born in 1897, Day knew about poverty firsthand. During her childhood, her father lost his job. Her family lived in a tenement house in Chicago. Eventually, the family's fortunes improved, but by then, Day had been awakened to the plight of the poor. Inspired by Upton Sinclair's novel *The Jungle*, she visited poor, immigrant neighborhoods in Chicago. After studying for two years at the University of Illinois, she moved to New York. She took a job as a reporter for the *Call*, a Socialist newspaper. She later worked for the *Masses*, another Socialist paper. In 1917 Day protested for woman suffrage (voting rights) at the White House and was jailed along with other protesters. In the 1920s, she continued working as a reporter and also found herself drawn to the Catholic faith. She officially joined the Catholic Church in 1927.

When the Depression hit, Day followed national events as a reporter. She reported on "Hunger Marches," a series of protests by unemployed people demanding that the government provide jobs, relief, health care, and housing. In 1932 she met a French writer named Peter Maurin. Together, they started a newspaper, the *Catholic Worker*. The paper preached a "social gospel." It taught that Christians had an obligation

DOROTHY DAY was a founder of the Catholic Worker Movement. She is seen here in 1934.

to care for the poor. To that end, Day and Maurin opened shelters for homeless men and women in New York City.

The Catholic Worker Movement spread. By 1936 thirty-three Catholic Worker shelters were operating around the United States. The movement also operated farms in New York and Pennsylvania. The Catholic Worker Movement advocated pacifism—even after the Japanese attacked Pearl Harbor, bringing the United States into World War II in 1941. In the 1950s, Day and her Catholic Worker colleagues protested against nuclear warfare. In the 1960s, they joined the civil rights movement, and in the 1970s, they supported striking farmworkers. Day died in 1980. Her *Catholic Worker* newspaper is still published.

■ "NO DEPRESSION IN HEAVEN"

Religion offered a solace to many people during the 1930s. The majority Christian population attended church on Sunday, while Jews worshipped on Friday night and Saturday. Americans of all faiths sent their children to religious schools and observed religious holidays. African Americans almost always attended all-black churches.

Worship services offered spiritual comfort to worried Americans in hard times, but some churches provided more direct help. In New York and other cities, the Catholic Worker Movement operated homeless shelters. In Los Angeles, California, radio preacher Aimee Semple McPherson ran a soup kitchen out of the Angelus Temple, part of her Foursquare Gospel Church. Homeless people could sleep in the temple if they had nowhere else to go. Some churches gave the homeless a heavy dose of preaching when they arrived for help, but McPherson's church gave only food, shelter, and hope.

A man named George Baker Jr., who called himself Father Divine, attracted many Americans to his Peace Mission movement in the 1930s. A black man, Father Divine attracted mostly black followers. He preached that people should be economically self-sufficient and not rely on welfare, yet he offered food to the hungry at his missions in New York City and elsewhere. Divine preached that he himself was God, a message that won him many enemies among the U.S. mainstream.

No matter how bad things got, the most devout Americans believed that a better life awaited them after death. The singing Carter Family, country musicians, promised audiences that there would be "No Depression in Heaven." Meanwhile, since a trip to heaven was generally in the future, religious Americans prayed that the Depression would soon end.

RADIO PREACHER AIMEE SEMPLE MCPHERSON (shown in the late 1920s) helped the poor from her Angelus Temple in Los Angeles.

47

GEORGE BAKER JR., KNOWN AS FATHER DIVINE helped his African American followers endure the Great Depression.

IN 1939, A NEW YORK WORLD'S FAIR GUIDE points to the Trylon and Perisphere, the emblems
of the exhibition. The World's Fair highlighted the products of tomorrow from around the world.

CHAPTER FOUR

THE WORLD OF TOMORROW:

TECHNOLOGY IN THE 1930s

The pace of life slowed in the 1930s. Whereas the 1920s had been a time of excitement—served up by fast cars, jazz music, and speakeasies—the 1930s was a time of anxiety. Worried about their pocketbooks, people were hesitant to buy the latest model Ford or the newest steam iron. But despite the Depression, technology chugged along in the 1930s. Businesses introduced new products to U.S. consumers.

At the DuPont Company, chemist Wallace H. Carothers experimented for years until he perfected nylon—a strong but flexible substance with hundreds of commercial and industrial uses. The first nylon products on the market were toothbrushes with nylon bristles. One year later, DuPont introduced nylon stockings, an instant hit when they reached de-

partment store shelves in late 1939. The 3M Company in Saint Paul, Minnesota, introduced Scotch tape in 1930. Made from a plasticlike substance called cellophane, the tape patched everything from torn dollar bills to cracked ceiling plaster.

Other new household products of the 1930s included Zippo lighters, electric shavers, and Windex glass cleaner. Only a lucky few were truly rich in the 1930s. But with Parker Brothers' Monopoly board game, introduced in 1933, anyone could be a real estate tycoon—if only for a few hours.

■ "MMM, MMM GOOD"

Food technology advanced steadily through the decade. Tired of baking biscuits from scratch? In 1931 a homemaker could buy Bisquick,

with all the ingredients premixed. For the perfect sandwich every time, home-makers could purchase presliced Wonder Bread. In the 1920s, inventor Clarence Birdseye had discovered that if fresh food was frozen quickly, it maintained its fresh taste and texture when heated later. After test marketing, the Birds Eye Company introduced a line of frozen food products—vegetables, fruits, fish, and meats—in 1934.

Many other (still-familiar) foods arrived on store shelves in the 1930s. They included Snickers and Three Musketeers candy bars, Hostess Twinkies, Fritos corn chips, Skippy peanut butter, Ritz crackers, and Spam canned meat. Familiar marketing slogans—Campbell Soup's "Mmm, Mmm Good," Wheaties' "Breakfast of Champions," and Wonder Bread's "Helps Build Strong Bodies Eight [later twelve] Ways"—also debuted in the 1930s.

For shopping convenience, A&P opened its first "supermarket"—with a full array of meats, produce, dairy, and grocery items—in Pennsylvania in 1936. To move more products down store aisles, and therefore move more dollars into cash registers, grocery chain magnate Sylvan Goldman created the first shopping cart in 1937.

Packaged foods, new technology, and larger stores combined to offer Americans of the 1930s a more varied and healthful diet than they had enjoyed previously. But food cost money, and money was in short supply during the Depression. Historians

A WOMAN SHOPS AT A SUPERMARKET in New York in 1939. Supermarkets were a new idea. They allowed shoppers to buy all their groceries at just one store.

Customers crowd a makeshift bar following the **REPEAL OF PROHIBITION** in 1933.

estimate that 40 percent of the U.S. population was underfed at one time or another during the 1930s. Brightening spirits for many was the fact that Prohibition—the ban on the manufacture and sale of alcohol—ended in 1933. For the first time since 1920, Americans could drink legally in restaurants and bars.

■ BLACK TOP

In 1930 the United States had 3 million miles (4.8 million km) of roads. However, more than 75 percent of these roads were unpaved. The New Deal made a dent in that percentage. Government programs allocated $3.3 billion to paving and improving the nation's roads. The programs helped drivers, of course,

and also put thousands of men to work on road crews.

As paved roadways expanded, the authorities grappled with keeping travelers safe. Traffic lights, first used in the 1910s and 1920s, came to more intersections in the 1930s. Municipalities posted safe speed limits. In Waco, Texas, in 1939, those limits were 45 miles (72 km) per hour for cars, 40 miles (64 km) per hour for buses, and 25 miles (40 km) per hour for big trucks. Oklahoma City installed the nation's first parking meter in 1935.

❝ The new word in style! The new car to buy! 1939 Studebaker ❞

—Colliers *magazine, automobile ad, 1939*

To move more and more cars greater distances, municipalities built new bridges, tunnels, and highways. In 1933 construction began on the Golden Gate Bridge across a strait in the San Francisco Bay. At 4,200 feet (1,280 meters), the rust-colored Golden Gate was then the world's longest suspension bridge.

■ SKYWARD

Cars were commonplace by the 1930s, but airplanes were still a novelty. In 1930 many Americans had never seen an airplane fly overhead—and certainly hadn't flown in one themselves. But that was changing. Government and business were discovering more uses for airplanes—from military reconnaissance (spying) to delivering mail and cargo. Companies such as the Curtiss-Wright Corporation and Grumman Aircraft were designing faster and safer airplanes—planes that would be capable of carrying many passengers for long distances.

Meanwhile, daredevil aviators set out to break new records for flying faster and farther. U.S. aviator Wiley Post was the first person to fly around the world solo. His 1933 flight took seven days, eighteen hours, and forty-nine minutes. U.S. movie producer and business tycoon (and aviation pioneer) Howard Hughes knocked the record down to three days, nineteen hours, and eight minutes when he circled the world in 1938.

To earthbound Americans, every flight was thrilling and aviators were heroes. Women flew as well as men—with record-setter Amelia Earhart earning the most fame among a host of female daredevils. In 1932 Earhart became the first woman to fly alone across the Atlantic Ocean. She and her copilot, Frederick Noonan, disappeared on an attempted flight around the world in 1937.

WILEY POST climbs out of the *Winnie May* after completing the first solo flight around the world in 1933.

AMELIA EARHART sits in the cockpit of her airplane in 1937.

A native of Atchison, Kansas, Amelia Earhart was adventurous from the start. As a little girl, she enjoyed "unladylike" pursuits such as climbing trees and hunting rats. After high school, she worked as a nurse's aide in Toronto, Canada. She later became a social worker. In 1920 a stunt pilot gave her a lift in his airplane. "By the time I had got two or three hundred feet [60 to 90 m] off the ground," she said, "I knew I had to fly."

Earhart took her first flying lesson in 1921 and soon saved enough money to buy her own plane. Shortly afterward, she set a women's altitude record by flying to 14,000 feet (4,267 m). Earhart kept working as a social worker and flew in her spare time.

In 1928 publicist George Putnam invited Earhart to join two male pilots on a flight across the Atlantic Ocean. After the successful flight—which made Earhart the first woman to fly the Atlantic—the three pilots returned to a ticker-tape parade in New York City and a White House reception with President Calvin Coolidge. After that, flying became a full-time job for Earhart. In 1929 she helped found a club called the Ninety-Nines, made up of female aviators.

Earhart's fame skyrocketed in 1932, when she became the first woman to fly solo across the Atlantic Ocean. Afterward, Congress awarded her the Distinguished Flying Cross, a military honor for heroism in flight. Earhart continued setting aviation records, for instance becoming the first person to fly solo from Hawaii to California in 1935.

The next challenge for Earhart was a flight around the world. On June 1, 1937, she and navigator Frederick Noonan took off from Miami, Florida, heading east. About 22,000 miles (35,398 km) later, Earhart and Noonan disappeared somewhere near Howland Island in the Pacific Ocean. The U.S. government searched 250,000 square miles (647,500 sq. km) of ocean trying to find the two flyers, with no luck. Most historians think that she and Noonan flew off course, ran out of fuel, and crashed into the ocean.

Douglas Corrigan also wanted to fly across the Atlantic Ocean, but because his airplane was old and unsafe, authorities told him no. They gave him the green light to fly from New York to California, but not to cross the ocean. On July 17, 1938, with two chocolate bars, a Boy Scout compass, and some maps torn from an atlas, Corrigan took off from Brooklyn, New York, in a thick fog. When he landed twenty-eight hours later, he wasn't in California but instead was in Dublin, Ireland. With a wink, Corrigan explained that he must have misread his compass. People everywhere laughed at the trick he had played. When he returned to the United States, "Wrong Way Corrigan" rode in a raucous ticker-tape parade through New York City.

By the late 1930s, the goal of long-distance passenger flights had become a reality. In 1939 Pan American Airways began flying passengers across the Atlantic Ocean. But a round-trip flight cost about $675—more than half the typical American's yearly earnings. So although long-distance airplane travel was possible, it was far from affordable in the 1930s. Most Americans who wanted to cross the ocean, for business or pleasure, trav-

eled by ocean liner. For overland trips, trains were economical.

For a short time, zeppelins, or airships, took people on luxurious long-distance flights. But the age of zeppelin travel came to an abrupt end in 1937 when a ship called the *Hindenburg* exploded in New Jersey after a transatlantic flight.

Although long-distance airplane travel was possible, it was far from affordable in the 1930s. Most Americans who wanted to cross the ocean, for business or pleasure, traveled by ocean liner.

■ "THE NEXT GREATEST THING"

In 1934 the United States Film Service, an agency of the U.S. government, set out to tell the nation about a new government program—a plan to bring electricity to U.S. farm families. The government wanted to promote the program in human terms. So it made a documentary film about a real farm family, the Parkinsons, and day-to-day work on their Ohio farm.

The film, called *Power and the Land,* showed what life was like without electricity. With only a kero-

sene lantern for lighting, Mr. Parkinson and his sons milked cows by hand before sunup. They cut wood by hand too, using axes and ripsaws. Mrs. Parkinson had to pump water by hand from a deep well and then haul it in buckets to the house. She cooked food over a hot and dirty woodstove and scrubbed dirty clothes against a washboard. After dinner, the family sat around at night reading, doing homework, and mending clothes—again by the dim light of a kerosene lamp.

The film showed audiences a grim reality for most rural Americans in the 1930s. While 85 percent of city dwellers had electricity in their homes by 1930, only 10 percent of U.S. farms were electrified. It wasn't profitable for power companies to run electric lines to widely scattered farms, so rural Americans kept scrubbing clothes, hauling water, and squinting to read in dim light while urban Americans enjoyed electric stoves, washing machines, and lights in every room.

Enter the New Deal and a program to provide power to rural areas of the United States. In 1934 an agency called the Rural Electrification Administration (REA) helped farmers form their own power cooperatives and string their own power lines. With low-interest loans from the REA, farmer-owned rural electric cooperatives spread across the nation. By 1940 about one-third of rural homes were wired for power (most of the rest were wired by the end of World War II).

Secretary of the Interior Harold Ickes *(left)* flips the switch to **TURN ON THE ELECTRIC FARM** in Dranesville, Virginia, in 1936. This model farm demonstrated how electricity could make farm chores easier.

On April 30, 1939, President Franklin Roosevelt stood amid a world of newly constructed buildings, statues, lights, fountains, and walkways. Before a giant crowd, he spoke into a series of microphones set up on a podium. "I hereby dedicate the World's Fair, the New York World's Fair, of 1939, and I declare it open to all mankind," Roosevelt announced.

As president, Roosevelt gave many speeches, of course, but this one was different. Not only was the speech broadcast via radio, it was also broadcast on television. The president's speech marked the beginning of regular TV broadcasts in the United States. (Although with only a few hundred television sets in the whole nation, it's unlikely that many people saw the speech.)

The 1939 World's Fair was a showcase for new ideas and new technology. Hundreds of companies, nations, and organizations set up exhibits at the fair to show visitors what the future might hold. In fact, the fair's motto was "Building the World of Tomorrow."

If the fair displays were any indication, the "world of tomorrow" was going to be bright. The Radio Corporation of America (RCA) showed off a television set—a huge wooden case with a tiny 7-inch (18-centimeter) picture tube. General Motors created its Futurama exhibit—a vision of the United States twenty years in the future), featuring placid suburbs and ten-lane superhighways. The Democracity exhibit, created by fair organizers, looked even further into the future, to 2039 and a world of towering skyscrapers, hydroelectric power plants, and parklike towns.

All types of futuristic cars, airplanes, labor saving devices, and other new inventions (FM radio, fluorescent lighting, robots, and air-conditioning) were on display, as well as artwork and fashions from around the world. Visitors rode amusement-park-style cars through some exhibits and traveled on moving walkways and stairways through others. In between, there was plenty of food to eat, musical shows, light shows, and other entertainments. After two April-to-October seasons, with a total of more than 45 million visitors, the fair shut down in 1940.

With electric wires running to their homes, farm families could use electric milking machines, water pumps, power saws, and all kinds of kitchen appliances. Although still difficult, farm life was no longer backbreaking. Those who received power under the REA had no end of praise for the program. One Tennessee farmer told his neighbors at a church service,

"Brothers and sisters, I want to tell you this. The greatest thing on earth is to have the love of God in your heart, and the next greatest thing is to have electricity in your house."

To meet the nation's growing power needs, the government also built a series of new hydroelectric dams in the 1930s. Near Las Vegas, Nevada, the Hoover Dam (for a while called the Boulder Dam when Herbert Hoover was widely unpopular) harnessed the

"Brothers and sisters, I want to tell you this. The greatest thing on earth is to have the love of God in your heart, and the next greatest thing is to have electricity in your house."

—Tennessee farmer, 1930s

power of the mighty Colorado River to generate electricity. The Grand Coulee Dam and the Bonneville Dam took their power from the Columbia River in Washington State. A New Deal agency called the Tennessee Valley Authority (TVA) built a series of dams and power plants on the Tennessee River and its tributaries in the southeastern United States in the 1930s. (The agency also addressed flood control, soil depletion, erosion, and other environmental issues.)

The dam projects not only generated power for the United States, they also gave jobs to the unemployed. What's more, they represented progress—the idea that the United States was moving forward with bigger and better technology.

THE HOOVER DAM was completed in 1935. This aerial photograph shows Lake Mead, which was created by the dam.

From left: Deputy Sheriff Charles McComb and attorney Samuel Leibowitz talk with seven of the nine DEFENDANTS IN THE SCOTTSBORO CASE: Roy Wright, Olen Montgomery, Ozie Powell, Willie Roberson, Eugene Williams, Charlie Weems, and Andy Wright.

CHAPTER FIVE

SIDELINED:
SOCIAL DIVISIONS IN THE 1930s

On March 25, 1931, a freight train on the Chattanooga Southern line sped through northern Alabama. As usual in the Depression years, the train carried dozens of unofficial passengers—homeless people riding the rails. Some had sneaked inside freight cars, while others clung to the sides of cars or rode on top. At one car, a young man on the roof stepped on the hand of another young man clinging to the side. A fight broke out between the two youths—one white and one black. "This is a white man's train," the white youth shouted. "You better get off. All you black bastards better get off!"

The fight soon spread to other cars. White riders and black riders wrestled and pummeled one another with fists. Finally, the black riders managed to throw almost all the white riders off the train.

The train continued down the line. When it stopped in the town of Paint Rock, a crowd of white men were waiting with guns. They'd gotten word of the brawl and wanted the black riders arrested for assault. The white men pulled nine black youths off the train, tied them up in a truck, and drove them to the sheriff in the nearby town of Scottsboro.

Around this time, two young white women came forward. They, too, were homeless. They, too, had been riding the train. The nine black youths had raped them at knifepoint, the young women claimed.

In the 1930s, racial hatred was fierce in the United States—especially in the South. Whites used both legal and illegal measures, including violence, to keep blacks from voting and exercising other rights. Blacks were not allowed to eat in restaurants with whites, attend school with whites, or use the same drinking fountains. One of the worst offenses, in the eyes of many white people, was sexual relations between a black man and a white woman.

In Scottsboro the accusations of rape by the two young women sent the townspeople into a rage. They surrounded the jail where the nine young men were being held, clamoring for the sheriff to hand over the prisoners.

The sheriff protected the prisoners from the mob, but the trials that followed were travesties. The two young women who made the rape charges told preposterous stories on the witness stand. The prosecution offered no evidence that the women had been raped—and, in fact, they hadn't been. Egged on by white men eager to prosecute the defendants, the two women had made up their story.

Despite the obvious false charges, eight of the nine defendants were found guilty and sentenced to death. "The people in the court cheered and clapped after the judge gave out with the [sentence]," one of the defendants remembered. "That courtroom was one big smiling white face." Outside the courthouse, a brass band played, and a crowd of ten thousand people cheered the verdict.

A MOB WAITS IN SCOTTSBORO, ALABAMA for the beginning of the trial of nine African American youths accused of raping two white women on a train.

The Scottsboro case focused the nation's attention on racial injustice and set the stage for the civil rights movement of later decades.

The Scottsboro case was a wakeup call for the nation. The trial clearly showed how much of the U.S. justice system was rigged against black defendants. In the North, the National Association for the Advancement of Colored People (NAACP) denounced the trial and others like it. Many mostly white organizations, such as the Communist Party USA and the American Civil Liberties Union, also protested the verdict. In 1932 the U.S. Supreme Court overturned the convictions, ruling that the defendants had not had adequate legal representation.

But the state of Alabama was determined to punish the nine young men. After a series of additional trials, four of them were convicted of rape and one was convicted of assault. Defense lawyers managed to save them from the death penalty. They served prison sentences instead.

The Scottsboro case was a tragedy for the men wrongly accused and convicted. Of course, it would have been far worse had the original death sentences held up in court. But for black people in the United States as a whole, the case was a turning point. It focused the nation's attention on racial injustice and set the stage for the civil rights movement of later decades.

■ COLOR LINES

In some ways, the 1930s were open season on minorities. Throughout the decade, Charles Coughlin, a Catholic priest who became a political commentator, viciously attacked Jews in his popular weekly radio broadcasts. In some California cities, Latinos weren't allowed to sit with whites in movie theaters, restaurants, and other public places. All along the West Coast, Asian Americans faced discrimination in housing and business. Other ethnic groups, such as immigrants from Italy, Poland, and other European nations, faced less overt discrimination, but they still endured frequent name calling and other slights from the nation's Anglo-American majority. To support one another, ethnic minorities usually stuck together—living in all-Jewish or all-Italian neighborhoods, for instance, and patronizing one another's businesses.

While most minority groups had it hard in the 1930s, African Americans

61

arguably suffered the most. "The Negro was born in depression," said Clifford Burke, a black man reflecting on the 1930s in the United States. He explained that for African Americans, times were always Depression-era tough, even before the stock market crashed.

In the 1930s, blacks faced discrimination in schooling, housing, and employment. Burke recalled that in urban areas, most black men worked as janitors, railroad porters (baggage carriers), and shoe shiners—because better jobs were off-limits to them. Black women mostly worked as maids and cooks for well-off white families. Sometimes black men landed factory jobs, but when companies laid off workers, blacks were the first ones to go.

In the rural South, slavery had ended almost seventy years earlier, but many African American families still lived no better than slaves. Most were sharecroppers or tenant farmers. Under various arrangements, they farmed someone else's land and paid a portion of their crops as rent. The system generally kept

SHARECROPPERS pick cotton in Mississippi in 1936.

them in debt to the landlord, poorly housed, poorly clothed, and hungry. As the Depression grew worse, hunger sometimes turned to starvation.

In southern states, police, politicians, sheriffs, landowners, and white terror groups such as the Ku Klux Klan enforced "Jim Crow"—a system of laws and practices that kept blacks and whites separated and ensured that blacks remained second-class citizens. The threat of violence always hung in the air. Even the slightest bit of defiance against white authority by a black man could get him a beating or much worse. Mobs of angry whites regularly lynched (murdered) black men in the most gruesome fashion. Routinely, black bodies ("strange fruit" in the words of a poem and of a song made famous by jazz singer Billie Holiday) were left hanging from trees.

The threat of violence always hung in the air. Even the slightest bit of defiance against white authority by a black man could get him a beating or much worse.

The situation outside the South was only slightly better. On Chicago's South Side, black families crowded into decrepit tenement buildings. Often an entire family lived in a single room, sharing a bathroom and a kitchen with neighbors. Some homes didn't have bathrooms at all. Others had no heat. Poor sanitation, poor medical care, and hunger combined to spread illness and disease through urban tenements.

Like all other Americans, black families used their wits and social networks to survive the Depression. A widespread tradition was the Saturday night "rent party." Hosts threw big bashes, with plenty of food, drink, and live music, and asked partygoers to make a contribution to help with the rent. In New York, well-known jazz musicians such as Fats Waller and Duke Ellington frequently played free at rent parties to help friends.

The New Deal was a lifesaver to some African Americans. WPA workers earned at least twelve dollars a week—twice what most black workers normally earned. Even so, in many government work programs, most jobs went to whites—even in places where blacks made up the majority of the population. And when they did get jobs, black New Deal workers were usually paid less than their white coworkers. Some whites complained

63

that blacks got government jobs at all. One shop clerk in Florida declared that blacks had no right to jobs "when there are white men who can do the work and are out of work."

One place where African Americans made great gains during the 1930s was in the socially liberal Roosevelt administration. FDR appointed many blacks to government posts. The leader among them was Mary McLeod Bethune, the president's special adviser on minority affairs and head of the Division of Negro Affairs at the National Youth Administration. An additional forty or so black men and women held high positions in federal offices. They were nicknamed the Black Cabinet. (The official cabinet is the president's group of top advisers.)

Socialists and Communists welcomed blacks into their organizations, although not many joined. Many labor unions, on the other hand, barred black members. The Brotherhood of Sleeping Car Porters was an almost all-black union, since almost all railroad porters were African American. Labor leader A. Philip Randolph had founded the union in 1925. In the 1930s, the union tussled with the Pullman Company, which employed the porters on its railroad sleeper cars. The brotherhood eventually earned many gains for porters.

MARY MCLEOD BETHUNE *(right)* visits with Eleanor Roosevelt in 1937. Bethune was a close friend of the First Lady as well as a part of Franklin D. Roosevelt's administration.

Standing just a little over 5 feet (1.5 m) tall, New York mayor Fiorello LaGuardia was a champion of the common people before, during, and after the 1930s. Born in New York in 1882, LaGuardia was the son of immigrants. His father had come to the United States from Italy. His mother was a Jewish immigrant from Austria-Hungary.

As a young man, LaGuardia worked for the U.S. Consular Service in Europe. In this job, he fought for fair treatment of immigrants coming to the United States. Returning to New York, LaGuardia worked at Ellis Island, the main port of entry for immigrants from Europe. LaGuardia knew five languages. He worked as a translator, speaking to immigrants in their native tongues when they arrived in New York. LaGuardia later became a lawyer and then a U.S. congressman. In Congress he fought on behalf of immigrants and labor unions.

In 1933 LaGuardia became mayor of New York City. He set to work cleaning up city government, which had been riddled with corruption. He also cracked down on organized crime. He worked with the Roosevelt administration to channel millions of New Deal dollars to New York City. The funds put people to work building parks, houses, schools, and hospitals. LaGuardia also oversaw the building of roads, tunnels, bridges, and an airport during his three terms as mayor. He was more than just an overseer, however. At different times

FIORELLO LAGUARDIA stood up for poor and working people throughout his long government career.

during his mayoral career, he directed city traffic, rushed to fires in a motorcycle sidecar, helped rescue a fireman pinned under a fallen beam, and conducted the New York Sanitation Department band.

During World War II, LaGuardia ran the Office of Civilian Defense. After the war, he directed the United Nations Relief and Rehabilitation Administration, which provided food, clothing, and shelter to millions of Europeans who had been displaced during wartime. LaGuardia died of cancer in 1947. New York's LaGuardia Airport is named in his honor.

65

The Prohibition era—1920 to 1933—led to an explosion of lawlessness in big U.S. cities. Big criminal gangs bought and sold illegal liquor. Rival gangs battled one another to control liquor supplies and markets. Crime kingpins such as Al Capone had a simple way of keeping the law off their back. They kept corrupt police and politicians on the payroll—paying them to ignore the illegal dealings.

By the early 1930s, most Americans were fed up with Prohibition. They wanted to drink legally, and they wanted the criminal gangs brought to justice. In 1931 federal agents managed to lock up Al Capone. Although he had been responsible for many murders, the government convicted him only of income tax evasion. Two years later, states ratified the Twenty-first Amendment to the Constitution, which repealed Prohibition. Without the illegal liquor business to fuel the criminal gangs, lawlessness died down.

Meanwhile, the federal government stepped up its efforts against criminals of all kinds. Headed by J. Edgar Hoover, the Federal Bureau of Investigation (FBI) hunted bank robbers, kidnappers, and other lawbreakers. In 1934 federal and local authorities shot bank robbers John Dillinger, Pretty Boy Floyd, and Bonnie and Clyde and locked up George "Machine Gun" Kelly. FBI agents—nicknamed G-men (government men)—became folk heroes to many Americans.

J. EDGAR HOOVER *(center)* was the first director of the Federal Bureau of Investigation.

■ HOME AND HEARTH

Most Americans followed a well-worn path in the early twentieth century. Like their parents before them, they got married and had children. But marriage rates declined dramatically in the 1930s, and so did the number of children per family. The reason was simple: people without money, people without jobs, and

people worried about losing jobs did not want to make a commitment to family life. They certainly didn't want to have large families with many children to feed. In fact, the 1930s saw the lowest birthrate of any decade ever in U.S. history. Couples practiced birth control to prevent unwanted pregnancies.

Large numbers of men abandoned their families during the 1930s. At first, men left to look for work in nearby cities—promising to send money or send for the whole family once a job had been found. But after weeks and months of searching with no success, some men left and never returned. Deserted wives had to care for children on their own. Like their vanished husbands, they searched the want ads, visited employment agencies, borrowed money, sold household items, and applied for relief. Women and children often ended up living in Hoovervilles, sleeping in church shelters, and even sneaking onto railroad cars.

People's health suffered. Even people with jobs and secure homes couldn't always afford to visit a doctor (or have a doctor visit, in this era of house calls). The poorest Americans, living with hunger and often in unsanitary housing, were vulnerable to diseases such as tuberculosis. Nevertheless, health-care professionals managed to keep people moderately healthy in the 1930s. They used then-new medical technology such as vaccines and X-rays to prevent and diagnose illness. In 1929 British scientist Alexander Fleming had discovered penicillin—the first antibiotic—but drugmakers had not yet figured out how to produce antibiotics in large quantities. Instead, doctors used less-effective sulfa drugs to treat bacterial infections. Life expectancy in the mid-1930s was about sixty years for men and sixty-four years for women.

■ WOMEN AT WORK

Work was gender-based in the 1930s. For instance, men drove trucks and worked construction. Women taught school and cleaned houses. Professional work—medicine, law, business, and engineering—was almost all done by men. Even New Deal jobs programs were segregated by sex. In the Civil Works Administration, for example, women worked as nurses, secretaries, seamstresses, and in other traditionally female occupations. In the WPA, they worked binding books, cooking, cleaning homes, canning foods, and caring for children.

67

Throughout the tough days of the Great Depression, one woman offered a solid shoulder for Americans to lean on. She was Eleanor Roosevelt, FDR's wife.

She was born Anna Eleanor Roosevelt in New York City in 1884. She was the niece of Theodore Roosevelt, who became U.S. president in 1901. As a teenager, Roosevelt attended a prestigious British boarding school. Returning to New York at the age of eighteen, she became active in social service work. She married her fifth cousin Franklin Roosevelt in 1905.

During World War I, Roosevelt worked in navy hospitals as a Red Cross volunteer. After the war, she became active in political and trade union groups. When FDR became president in 1932, Eleanor also took the spotlight. She traveled extensively, visited New Deal projects, advised her husband on national affairs, gave lectures, and wrote books.

Starting in 1936, she wrote a six-day-a-week newspaper column called My Day. Some My Day pieces contained chatty reflections on Roosevelt's pastimes and family life. Some discussed New Deal programs, while others addressed international affairs.

Many Americans—especially the very poor—revered Eleanor Roosevelt, just as they did her husband. Historians estimate that during the 1930s, more than one thousand Americans wrote letters to Eleanor every week.

Roosevelt was sometimes outspoken, especially for a woman of her era. She championed the rights of women, minorities, and the poor. In 1939 the Daughters of the American Revolution—an organization whose members traced their heritage back to the fight for U.S. independence—refused to allow black singer Marian Anderson to sing in Constitution Hall in Washington, D.C. In protest, Roosevelt resigned from the organization. She then arranged for Anderson to give a concert for more than seventy-five thousand people at the Lincoln Memorial.

Roosevelt remained politically active during World War II. FDR died in 1945, but Eleanor did not slow down. From 1945 to 1962, the year of her death, she held various positions at the United Nations.

ELEANOR ROOSEVELT *(right)* and Labor Secretary FRANCES PERKINS attend an awards dinner in Washington, D.C., in 1934.

Like black New Deal workers, women got lower pay than their male counterparts. On WPA work projects, men earned five dollars a day. Women got three dollars.

Many men opposed giving jobs to women at all, espousing the traditional belief that women should work in the home while men held paying jobs. This attitude was widespread. In fact, more than 75 percent of U.S. school districts banned the employment of married women teachers in the 1930s. If a woman had a husband, the argument went, he should support her. A 1936 Gallup Poll asked Americans if women should work if their husbands had jobs, and 82 percent of respondents said no. Thus when the government specifically gave jobs to women in the face of widespread male unemployment, many men complained.

" Please do not think this does not cause a great feeling of shame to me to have to ask for old clothing. I am so badly in need of a summer coat and under things and dresses. . . . Please send me anything you may have on hand . . . which you don't care to wear yourself."

—*Iowa woman's letter to First Lady Eleanor Roosevelt, 1936*

Some unions welcomed female members, while others barred them. Most women participated in unions as part of "women's auxiliaries," groups made up of wives, sisters, and daughters of male members. The women marched on picket lines and cooked food for men holed up in factories during sit-down strikes.

Women played a big role in the Roosevelt administration. Labor Secretary Frances Perkins was the first female cabinet member in U.S. history. Eleanor Roosevelt, more active than any First Lady before her, played a major part in steering her husband's New Deal decisions. She also offered encouragement to women in the face of economic hard times. "The women know," she wrote in 1933, "that life must go on and that the needs of life must be met, and it is their courage and determination which, time and again, have pulled us through worse crises than the present one."

THE FEDERAL WRITERS PROJECT (FWP) produced these
volumes for the American Guide Series in the late 1930s.

CHAPTER SIX

THE PRINTED PAGE:
LITERATURE OF THE 1930s

The Depression hit all industries hard, and publishing was no exception. In the first four years after the stock market crash, book sales tumbled by half. Authors who had made money from royalties—payments based on how well their books sold—faced drastic cuts in income. Magazines brought in less and less money from advertisers, so they had to cut costs—paying staff and writers less. Between 1930 and 1935, almost half of all U.S. newspapers went out of business. Thousands of reporters took to the streets looking for work.

Many of these out-of-work writers caught a break in 1935, when the government created Federal Project Number One—a New Deal program to provide work for artists, writers, actors, and musicians. The writers' division was called the Federal Writers Project. From 1935 to 1939, it hired more than sixty-six hundred writers, editors, and researchers to create a variety of publications: guidebooks to the U.S. states, cities, and regions; oral histories of former African American slaves and other Americans; folklore and folk song collections; radio scripts; pamphlets; articles; and scholarly studies. The guidebooks, called the American Guide Series, were the most successful of the FWP publications. Much of the writing was vivid and

lyrical. Consider this description of the Wyoming countryside, crafted by an uncredited FWP writer:

Here in Wyoming's great spaces, winds blow over prairies and mountains, sending Russian thistle and other tumbleweeds bounding for miles, piling snow in deep drifts or melting it like magic; barbed wire or buck fences stretch for miles; zigzagging snow fences apparently lead nowhere, but actually guard your path; the atmosphere is so clear that mountains far away seem near, and stars shine so brilliantly they look within reach; columns of train smoke rise on far horizons; streamlined trains flash through the sage; mainline ships thunder overhead.

It's no surprise that the FWP turned out high-quality writing. Many talented authors worked in its ranks. John Cheever, Richard Wright, Ralph Ellison, Saul Bellow, and other soon-to-be-well-known novelists worked for the FWP early in their careers. Like the author who described Wyoming, these writers received no bylines on their FWP work, but they did get a paycheck of twenty to twenty-five dollars a week—a godsend to the previously unemployed.

■ FUTURE CLASSICS

Even with the downturn in publishing, Americans still loved a good page-turner, and some of the greatest novels of the twentieth century arrived in bookstores during the 1930s. The decade's premier writer was William Faulkner. After launching his literary career in the 1920s, he published a string of powerful novels in the following

WILLIAM FAULKNER won the Nobel Prize in Literature in 1949.

In June 1939, the Simon and Schuster Company announced the birth of a new product line that would "revolutionize New York's reading habits." It was the low-cost, pocket-sized paperback book. The company's new paperback division, called Pocket Books, launched with ten titles: *Wuthering Heights* by Emily Bronte, *Topper* by Thorne Smith, *Lost Horizon* by James Hilton, *The Bridge of San Luis Rey* by Thornton Wilder, *The Murder of Roger Ackroyd* by Agatha Christie, and five tragic plays by William Shakespeare. Pocket's logo was Gertrude, a plump kangaroo who wore reading glasses and carried a book tucked conveniently inside her pouch.

The 4.5-by-6.5-inch (11.5-by-16.5 cm) books were indeed small enough to fit in a coat pocket. At twenty-five cents each, they were much cheaper than hardcovers, which sold for about two to three dollars during the 1930s. Readers had to visit bookstores to buy hardcover books, but Pocket placed its paperbacks at drugstores, department stores, and newsstands, as well as bookstores. By making books more available and affordable, Pocket introduced the world's greatest literature to many people who had never read it before.

The books caught on like wildfire. Robert de Graff, who headed Pocket Books, recalled the day the paperbacks went on sale: "At four o'clock in the afternoon, the phone started ringing, and it rang and rang—these were people calling up for re-orders and the phone was so busy, messengers began arriving, and they said, 'We're all sold out, we need some more books.'"

decade: *As I Lay Dying* (1930), *Sanctuary* (1931), *Light in August* (1932), *Pylon* (1935), *Absalom, Absalom!* (1936), *The Unvanquished* (1938), and *The Wild Palms* (1939). Several of these works are set in the fictional Yoknapatawpha County, modeled after Faulkner's hometown of Oxford, Mississippi. Examining difficult topics such as morality, race relations, and family conflict, Faulkner soon joined the ranks of the leading authors of the twentieth century.

Another literary giant of the 1930s was Ernest Hemingway. Like Faulkner, he first found fame in the 1920s. In the 1930s, he published both fiction and nonfiction. In the novel *To Have and Have Not* (1937), the chief character finds it impossible to earn an honest living in Depression-era Florida. He becomes an outlaw who smuggles rum and Chinese immigrants into Cuba. In the late 1930s,

Hemingway went to Spain to report on the Spanish Civil War (1936–1939). He used this conflict as the setting for his 1940 novel *For Whom the Bell Tolls.*

Pearl Buck was a U.S.-born author who spent most of her life in China. She came to acclaim with *The Good Earth* (1931), which chronicles the struggles of Wang Lung, a Chinese peasant. The novel won the 1932 Pulitzer Prize. A prolific writer, Buck published seven other novels in the 1930s. During her long career, she also wrote short stories, essays, and biographies.

John Steinbeck, another 1930s literary standout, set many of his works in Salinas, California, the farming community where he was born. In several books, Steinbeck examined the struggles of Depression-era farmworkers. For instance, *In Dubious Battle* (1936) is a novel about striking fruit pickers. *Of Mice and Men* (1937) tells the story of two ranch hands who dream of owning their own land. In 1939 Steinbeck published *The Grapes of Wrath,* his master-work. This epic novel depicts the desperate Joad family fleeing from the dust bowl in Oklahoma—only to find deeper despair in the fruit fields of California. The book won the 1940 Pulitzer Prize.

■ SOMETHING FOR EVERYONE

Writers churned out books for every taste in the 1930s. The Nancy Drew mystery series, aimed at teen readers, debuted in 1930 and immediately won avid fans. Laura Ingalls Wilder published her first Little House book, *Little House in the Big Woods,* in 1932. This children's favorite recounts Wilder's girl-hood on the U.S. frontier. She followed that with *Little House on the Prairie* (1935), *On the Banks of Plum Creek* (1937), and *On the Shores of Silver Lake* (1939), with additional books in the series in the 1940s.

LAURA INGALLS WILDER signs a copy of one of her books in the 1930s.

Zora Neale Hurston was a multifaceted writer who produced her best work in the 1930s. An African American, Hurston was born in Notasulga, Alabama, in 1891. As a toddler, she moved with her family to all-black Eatonville, Florida. Hurston enjoyed a contented childhood in Eatonville, but with the death of her mother in 1904, her family life became more difficult. Hurston left Florida for Baltimore, Maryland, and eventually settled in New York City. There, in the mid-1920s, she found herself in the center of the Harlem Renaissance—a time of literary and artistic outpouring in New York's African American community.

Hurston began writing plays and short stories. She enrolled in New York's Barnard College, where she studied anthropology. She put this training to work in the early 1930s, traveling to Louisiana to collect African American folk songs and folklore. She gathered the songs and stories into a 1935 collection called *Mules and Men*.

In the late 1930s, Hurston joined the Federal Writers Project, where she did additional folklore collecting, this time in Florida. At the same time, Hurston also wrote fiction. *Their Eyes Were Watching God* (1937) is her best known of three novels from the 1930s. *Tell My Horse*, published in 1938, was another folklore study—this one centering on the folk customs of Haiti and Jamaica.

Hurston published her autobiography,

ZORA NEALE HURSTON enjoyed her greatest literary success in the 1930s.

Dust Tracks on a Road, in 1942. Her last novel, *Seraph on the Suwanee*, appeared in 1948. Despite critical acclaim for her work, Hurston never made much money from her writing. In the 1950s, she made a meager living teaching and writing magazine and newspaper articles. She died in 1960 in Florida, after suffering a stroke. She was nearly penniless at her death and was buried in an unmarked grave.

In 1973 the African American writer Alice Walker arranged to place a marker on Hurston's grave. Walker and other young writers also helped win Hurston the acclaim that had eluded her in her lifetime.

For those who loved detective stories, Dashiell Hammett offered *The Maltese Falcon* (1930), *The Glass Key* (1931), and *The Thin Man* (1934), featuring fictional detectives Sam Spade, Ned Beaumont, and Nick and Nora Charles, respectively. In 1939 Raymond Chandler introduced Philip Marlowe, the classic "hard-boiled" detective, in *The Big Sleep*.

Gone with the Wind (1936), by Margaret Mitchell, is a sweeping Civil War epic. It features the romance between Southern belle Scarlet O'Hara and the swaggering Rhett Butler, set against the backdrop of the war-ravaged American South of the 1860s. The best-selling book won the 1937 Pulitzer Prize. It became an equally successful movie in 1939.

> **"With her first novel, Miss Mitchell proves herself a staggeringly gifted storyteller, empowered . . . with some secretion in the blood for effortlessly inventing and prolonging excitement. Her vast chronicle of the South during and after the Civil War is perhaps more than a novel, perhaps a whole library in itself."**

—New Yorker *magazine review of* Gone with the Wind, *1936*

Most best sellers of the 1930s were fictional works, but one work of nonfiction sold along with the best of them. It was Dale Carnegie's *How to Win Friends and Influence People,* published in 1936. Carnegie began his career as a salesman and later taught public speaking to businesspeople. In *How to Win Friends,* he advised readers: "Believe that you will succeed, and you will." In the thick of the Great Depression, this was advice that many Americans were eager to follow. Carnegie's book sold in the millions.

■ BLACK AND WHITE

Reading—especially romance novels or detective novels—could provide a distraction from life's pain and suffering in the Depression years. But several writers of the 1930s didn't shy away from that suffering. Richard Wright spelled

out the brutal treatment of blacks in the southern United States in the fictional *Uncle Tom's Children* (1938). In the following decade, Wright further explored the African American experience through both fiction and nonfiction.

James Agee also wrote both fiction and nonfiction. His most well-known work, *Let Us Now Praise Famous Men*, examines the lives of three white tenant farm families in Alabama. Agee and photographer Walker Evans, on assignment for *Fortune* magazine, lived with the families in the summer of 1936. *Fortune* never printed the resulting text and photographs. Instead, the material appeared in book form in 1941. Evans's photos captured the gaunt faces, threadbare clothing, and ramshackle homes of the three families—the Rickettses, Woodses, and Gudgers—while Agee described their lives in great detail. Reviewers called *Let Us Now Praise Famous Men* a masterpiece. Like the *Grapes of Wrath*, it showed ordinary Americans coping with extraordinary hardship.

The Woods family *(below)* was one of three struggling families chronicled in James Agee's **LET US NOW PRAISE FAMOUS MEN.**

The interior of Radio City Music Hall in New York City is a
classic example of the ART DECO STYLE of the 1930s.

CHAPTER SEVEN

STREAMLINED:
ART AND DESIGN OF THE 1930s

79

If everyone was broke in the 1930s, you wouldn't know it to look at Radio City Music Hall. Part of the Rockefeller Center complex in New York City, the music hall was compared to a palace when it opened in 1932. With its sweeping arched ceiling, shimmering gold stage curtain, curving stairways, and elegant marble and gold-foil decorations, it was the epitome of opulence.

Radio City Music Hall was built in the art deco style. Emerging in Paris, France—the epicenter of fashion—art deco stood for wealth, sophistication, and high class. The style hit the United States in the late 1920s, when money was flowing freely. Even in the 1930s, when the money dried up, U.S. designers and architects stuck to art deco.

The style featured zigzags and other geometric shapes, curved lines, and sleek forms. Much jewelry, furniture, textiles, and housewares of the 1930s boasted art deco styling. New York skyscrapers such as the Chrysler Building (completed in 1930) and the Empire State Building (1931) had art deco elements both inside and out.

Art deco streamlining reached its peak with industrial design. Cars, airplanes, and passenger trains were created with smooth, teardrop-shaped surfaces—which allowed air to slip past them more easily, thus increasing the vehicles' speed. Streamlining wasn't limited to

BURLINGTON RAILROAD'S DENVER ZEPHYR was a streamlined passenger train that ran from Chicago to Denver, Colorado, starting in 1936.

vehicles. Product designer Raymond Loewy even created a teardrop-shaped pencil sharpener in 1933.

French art deco started with luxurious, organic raw materials such as hardwood, stone, and crystal. U.S. art deco was more industrially oriented. U.S. designers worked with chrome, stainless steel, and molded plastics. These materials spoke of efficiency, mass production, and most of all speed. "Speed is the cry of our era," declared designer Norman Bel Geddes, "and greater speed one of the goals of tomorrow."

■ TOP HATS AND TAILS

Those who could afford it—and even those who couldn't—wanted to look good in the 1930s. In fact, rich or poor, everyone was expected to maintain certain standards of dress. This was a formal decade. Men stood up and removed their hats when a woman entered the room. They wore ties at meals and even wore suits and ties to ball games. Women wore dresses and skirts (although slacks were slowly coming into fashion) and wore gloves and hats when they went out to dine, shop, or visit friends. In her *New Book of Etiquette* (1937), manners maven Emily Post outlined the proper attire for every occasion. She

told theatergoers: "At the highest-type evening performance in New York, especially when the play has not been on very long, a lady wears a semi-evening dress, a gentleman a 'tuxedo.' Full dress is always worn at smart theaters in London but is seldom worn in New York except by those who are going to a party later."

Free-spirited women of the 1920s had gone in for short skirts and boyish haircuts. Women of the 1930s returned to a more elegant, feminine look. Hemlines dropped back to the ankle, and necklines also plunged. Designers gussied up dresses with ruffles, scallops, pleats, bows, and puffy sleeves. Wealthy women wore fur capes, coats, stoles, and wraps. Women's shoes featured high heels, rounded toes, ankle straps, and buckles. Most women's hats had wide brims, although berets and pillbox styles were also popular. The smart woman carried a beaded or mesh handbag. She wore her hair short and neatly curled.

Men also looked sharp in the 1930s. They slicked back their hair with petroleum jelly and kept their shoes shined. A suit (with a waistcoat, or vest) was proper attire for an office job. Gas station attendants, delivery men, repairmen, ushers, and other service workers wore company-issued uniforms. In high society, men wore striped trousers, silk coats, and top hats for special occasions. At nightclubs and theaters, silk and slick hair meshed well with the sleek chrome and curves of art deco style.

Actors Gloria Swanson and Herbert Marshall appear at a Beverly Hills film premiere in **CLASSIC 1930s FASHION**.

But the Depression was on. How could people look good without money? Many couldn't. They mended and patched old clothes, but repairs would go only so far. Unemployed Americans eventually wore holes in their shoes. Their coats became dirty and tattered. However shiny and sleek, art deco and high fashion couldn't disguise that many Americans were struggling—even starving—in the 1930s.

■ REALISTS AND REGIONALISTS

While product and fashion designers put a high gloss on the 1930s, many fine artists took a different approach. Artists of the realist school tried to show 1930s life without the glitz and glitter. Ben Shahn, a Lithuanian Jewish immigrant, was concerned with political injustice and the plight of downtrodden Americans. His

paintings, drawings, and prints of the 1930s depict strikers, workers, and the poor. Edward Hopper made pictures of ordinary people, ordinary homes, and ordinary U.S. streets. His paintings did not send overt political messages, but they nevertheless captured the sadness that pervaded the Depression era in the United States. Jacob Lawrence filled his canvases with images of African Americans at work and at home, as well as scenes from African American history. His most acclaimed work was a sixty-panel series called *Migration of the Negro*. It depicts the great migration of blacks from the rural South to northern cities after World War I. Lawrence did not shy away from showing the worst racism endured by blacks— even images of lynching.

EDWARD HOPPER painted *Macomb's Dam Bridge (right)* in 1935.

Alexander Calder, one of the leading artists of the 1930s, didn't concern himself with the politics or economics of the Great Depression. Instead, Calder made playful sculptures. He even invented a new art form—the mobile, or moving sculpture.

Alexander Calder was born in Philadelphia in 1898. His father was a sculptor, and his mother was a painter. By the age of eleven, Alexander was making his own sculptures—animals cut from sheets of brass and then bent into shape.

After high school, Calder studied engineering. He worked as an engineer for several years but found himself pulled more toward art. In 1923 he moved to New York City and enrolled in the Art Students League. He also worked as an illustrator for the *National Police Gazette*. In 1925 the *Gazette* sent Calder to sketch pictures of a circus—an assignment that inspired him to create a work called *Cirque Calder* (the Calder Circus). It was an assemblage of tiny circus performers, animals, and props made out of wire, leather, cloth, and other materials. Calder manipulated the pieces to present a circus show for friends.

In 1931, while working in Paris, Calder created his first moving sculptures, which moved by means of cranks and motors. The famous French artist Marcel Duchamp dubbed them *mobiles*, meaning "movable." Calder next made mobiles that moved without mechanical help. They were precisely

ALEXANDER CALDER poses next to one of his creations in 1936.

balanced assemblages of wood, string, metal, and wire that hung from the ceiling or sat on stands. The pieces of each sculpture moved independently of one another, pushed by air currents.

Back in the United States, Calder made mobiles as well as stabiles—nonmoving sculptures. Some of his works were enormous outdoor metal sculptures standing several stories high. Calder worked until his death in 1976.

Some of Calder's mobiles, such as *.125* in John F. Kennedy Airport in New York City, hang in public places. But people who might never see a real Calder up close can still enjoy the artwork he invented. In modern times, lots of people hang mobiles in their homes and workplaces.

Joining the realists in the spotlight in the 1930s were the regionalists, artists whose work captured the flavor of distinct regions of the United States. Grant Wood painted scenes of an idyllic rural United States, peopled by stoic, hardworking farmers. His most famous picture, *American Gothic* (1930), shows a man and woman—possibly a father and daughter—standing before a farmhouse. The bald-headed man wears overalls, a dark jacket, and steel-rimmed spectacles. He grips a pitchfork in one hand. The woman, her hair pulled back tightly behind her head, wears an apron over a somber

Grant Wood first exhibited **AMERICAN GOTHIC** in 1930 at the Art Institute of Chicago.

black dress. Both characters have long, gloomy faces. The building behind them is a typical Iowa farmhouse, but it has a Gothic-style window more commonly found on a church. Art historians have long argued about the painting's meaning. Was Wood making fun of old-fashioned country people or praising them? Whatever its meaning, *American Gothic* soon became a classic. With the nation shifting to a more mechanized, urban way of life in the 1930s and with farm families under assault from drought and dust, the picture captured a lifestyle and an attitude that seemed to be quickly fading.

Thomas Hart Benton also painted the midwestern scene—especially his home state of Missouri. Benton's works are populated by muscular, raw-boned farmers and craftspeople. His works often show scenes from U.S. history. In 1936 Benton completed *A Social History of the State of Missouri,* a series of large murals in the Missouri state capitol building in Jefferson City. The paintings show pioneers,

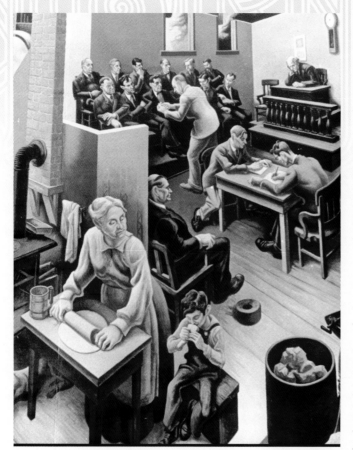

This detail of Thomas Hart Benton's *A SOCIAL HISTORY OF THE STATE OF MISSOURI* mural shows the interiors of a one-room Missouri farmhouse and a courthouse.

farmers, politicians, city dwellers, and famous Missourians—both real (Jesse James) and fictional (Huck Finn). Vivid colors, intricate detail, and people in motion are hallmarks of this and all of Benton's work.

■ FEDERAL ART

The Federal Art Project (FAP; part of Federal Project Number One) and its precursor, the Public Works of Art Project (PWAP), hired artists to create murals and other artwork to adorn public buildings and public spaces. In theory, the programs were designed to enrich the general public by exposing them to fine art. In reality, the programs were meant to help unemployed artists. "They've got to eat just like other people," argued New Deal administrator Harry Hopkins when some critics complained about supporting artists. The PWAP hired about thirty-six hundred artists, while the later FAP employed another four thousand. As with the Federal Writers Project, some soon-to-be-famous names—most notably abstract painter Jackson Pollock—made art on the government payroll.

Using both watercolors and oils, PWAP and FAP painters created portraits, landscapes, cityscapes, and historical images. The paintings were then distributed to decorate the walls of schools, libraries, hospitals, and government agencies. PWAP and FAP sculptors made busts and statues for parks and other public places.

In addition, graphic artists created more than one million government

A **WPA POSTER** advertises a show of WPA paintings.

posters, most of them with a social or public health message. "John is not really dull [dumb]—he may only need his eyes examined," declared one such poster. It showed a concerned mother fretting over her underachieving son. The words were arranged from large to small, like letters on an optometrist's examination chart. "The solution to infant mortality [death] in the slums—better housing," another poster said. It showed a run-down tenement with the specter of Death on one side and a clean new housing project on the other. Other federal posters promoted national parks, New Deal projects, educational programs, community events, and theatrical performances. Most of the posters featured plain block lettering and simple graphic elements, but a few of them were real art deco knockouts, with bold geometric designs and stylish curves.

The federal art programs were probably most famous for their murals—many of them created for U.S. post offices. The murals stirred up some controversy. At the time, the leading muralist in the United States was Mexican painter Diego Rivera. His creations for Rockefeller Center, the Detroit Institute of Arts, and other institutions featured scenes of toiling workers and even some Communist symbols. (Upset by a portrait of Communist leader Vladimir Lenin in the Rockefeller Center mural, the Rockefeller family had the whole mural destroyed.) The federal muralists followed Rivera's lead, with scenes of hardworking laborers that looked, to some, like pro-union, antibusiness propaganda. Not surprisingly, some U.S. leaders voiced their opinion that the New Deal art programs had been infiltrated by Communists. But the murals remained and can still be seen in many U.S. post offices and public buildings.

■ LOOK

Photographers were hard at work during the 1930s. Some took pictures for daily newspapers, snapping scenes of politicians, parades, and pageant winners. Others worked for Hollywood studios, capturing glamour shots of Jean Harlow, Joan Crawford, and other screen sirens. Still others made photos for *Look, Life, Pic, Click,* and other picture-heavy magazines. Lewis Hine took his camera hundreds of feet in the air to document workers erecting the Empire State Building. By the 1930s, photography was more than eighty years old. Americans were used to seeing photographs everywhere—from billboards to art gallery walls to high school yearbooks. Many families had their own cameras for taking snapshots.

"To see life; see the world."

—Life *magazine's mission statement, after its relaunching as a photo magazine in 1936*

Documentary photography played a big role in the 1930s, thanks primarily to the Farm Security Administration (FSA). This New Deal program was designed to help poor farmers. It loaned them money for new equipment, trained them in farming techniques, ran camps for dust bowl refugees, and moved some families to

collective farms, owned and managed by the government. The FSA also hired photographers, both to document its work and to focus attention on the plight of rural Americans.

To take the pictures, FSA Information Division head Roy Stryker signed some of the premier photographers of the era: Dorothea Lange, Arthur Rothstein, Walker Evans, Berenice Abbott, Russell Lee, Carl Mydans, Gordon Parks, and others. For the rest of the decade and into the 1940s, they shot scenes of people and the land: sharecroppers, fruit pickers, and dust bowl migrants. And their subjects soon went way beyond rural America and the FSA programs. The photographers also captured images of steelworkers, autoworkers, union organizers, and men looking for work, dam construction, big-city streets, factories, and everything in between.

The FSA photographers captured some of the era's most wrenching scenes of poverty and despair. One picture, Dorothea Lange's "Migrant Mother" (part of a larger series), is probably the most widely printed image of the Great Depression. The photograph shows homeless migrant Florence Owens Thompson and her children. Thompson's face is lined. Her eyes are filled with worry; her brow is furrowed. She holds an infant in her lap while two other children hide their faces against her neck. Many years after she took the picture, Lange remembered the scene:

"MIGRANT MOTHER" by Dorothea Lange was taken in California in 1936.

I saw and approached the hungry and desperate mother, as if drawn by a magnet. I do not remember how I explained my presence or my camera to her,

In the early twentieth century, kids loved to read newspaper comic strips. Artist Joe Shuster remembered, "In those days, color comics were published on a large scale. [Newspapers] would devote an entire page to one comic, usually with vivid colors, very bright, vivid colors."

Newspapers introduced many popular comic characters in the 1930s. Blondie arrived in U.S. newspapers in 1930, Dick Tracy showed up in 1931, and Li'l Abner debuted in 1934. Dell Publishing produced the first official "comic book," *Famous Funnies,* in 1934. Soon, characters such as Popeye and Flash Gordon were featured in comic books as well as newspaper strips.

In the mid-1930s, Joe Shuster and his friend Jerry Siegel created a comic strip about a baby from the planet Krypton, adopted by the Kent family after traveling to Earth via rocket ship. The baby, of course, grew up to be Superman. After several years of shopping their story around, Shuster and Siegel finally sold it to DC Comics.

Superman made his thirteen-page debut in DC's Action Comics series in June 1938. The new superhero was an instant hit. Within months, Superman had his own comic book and his own newspaper strip, with plans under way for a radio series, animated cartoons, and movies.

but I do remember she asked me no questions. I made five exposures, working closer and closer from the same direction. I did not ask her name or her history. She told me her age, that she was thirty-two. She said that they had been living on frozen vegetables from the surrounding fields, and birds that the children killed. She had just sold the tires from her car to buy food. There she sat in that lean-to tent with her children huddled around her, and seemed to know that my pictures might help her, and so she helped me. There was a sort of equality about it.

Roy Stryker was a brilliant publicist. He made sure that "Migrant Mother" and other FSA photographs made their way into newspapers, magazines, and government reports. The widely distributed images helped drum up support for FSA and other New Deal programs. They reminded more fortunate Americans that many others were hungry and needed their help.

MGM'S SENSATI
"THE WIZARD OF
JUDY GARLAND   FRANK
BERT LAHR   JACK
A. SCHULTE
TELEPHONE BOOTHS
CIGARS A. SCHULTE CIGARS
CIGA

Hundreds gather outside of a theater for the New York City
premiere of *THE WIZARD OF OZ* in 1939.

CHAPTER EIGHT

STAGE DOOR:
DRAMATIC ARTS OF THE 1930s

Movies were just a few decades old in the 1930s, and "the talkies" were quite new, having been introduced in 1927. Americans of the 1930s loved going to the movies. At mid-decade, about 60 percent of citizens went to the movie theater at least once a week. Tickets cost twenty cents for adults and ten cents for kids. For this admission price, audiences watched two feature films, plus a newsreel, a cartoon, a short film, and coming attractions before the features.

In the 1930s, Hollywood movie studios operated like factories. They employed hundreds of stars, supporting players, and character actors (who played certain types, such as the kindly Irish cop, the snobby society woman, or the wisecracking secretary). Actors worked long, hard hours. Before he became a star, Cary Grant appeared in eight movies in just one year (1932). A big studio could make a movie in just one week, or about fifty movies a year.

Some films of the 1930s dealt directly with Depression-era themes, but most movies of the decade gave viewers a temporary escape from the Depression. The much-beloved *Gone with the Wind* (1939; based on Margaret Mitchell's novel) swept moviegoers into the long-gone Civil War South. *The Wizard of Oz* (also 1939) took audiences into even less familiar territory—the Land of Oz, somewhere "over the rainbow."

91

■ LAUGHING MATTER

Moviegoers who wanted to laugh could always count on the great movie comedians of the 1930s. Leading the pack was W. C. Fields, who usually played a bumbler, a con man, or some other kind of troublemaker in his twenty-plus 1930s comedies. With his big round nose, snide remarks, and silly physical comedy, Fields kept movie audiences in stitches.

Brash, blond, and curvaceous, Mae West always played a sexy—and funny—seductress on-screen. Fans guffawed when she dropped lines such as "It's not the men in your life that counts—it's the life in your men" (from *I'm No Angel,* 1933). West's humor could be a little risqué for the 1930s—at least that's what the censors thought. Often, censors cut the most sexually suggestive lines and scenes from her movies.

The Marx Brothers—who used the stage names Groucho, Chico, and Harpo (sometimes joined by their brother Zeppo)—released a string of brilliant comedies in the 1930s. These included *Duck Soup* (1933), *A Night at the Opera* (1935), and *A Day at the Races* (1937). The brothers played every scene for laughs. Cigar-puffing Groucho raised his bushy eyebrows while delivering zingy wisecracks and put-downs, Chico talked with a fake Italian accent, while Harpo (who played the harp) never spoke.

MAE WEST appeared in eight major motion pictures in the 1930s.

In the 1930s, German-born actress Marlene Dietrich captivated U.S. audiences with her husky singing voice, stunning good looks, and exotic German accent. Born in Berlin in 1901, Dietrich trained to be a violinist but switched to acting after injuring her hand. In the 1920s, she attended drama school and landed small roles in German theater and silent films.

In 1929 the German director Josef Von Sternberg cast her as the lead in *Der Blaue Engel (The Blue Angel).* In this film, she sang her signature song, "Falling in Love Again." When the film played in the United States, moviemakers recognized Dietrich's star potential. In 1930 Dietrich moved to Hollywood and signed with Paramount Studios.

With Paramount, Dietrich appeared in *Morocco, Blonde Venus, Shanghai Express, The Devil Is a Woman,* and other dramas. Von Sternberg, who had also moved to Hollywood, directed most of her films. Dietrich often played a cabaret singer, which allowed her to show off her alluring singing voice. Von Sternberg used moody lighting and shadows to make Dietrich appear sexy and mysterious. In *Morocco* she wore a man's suit and top hat, a costume that became her trademark.

In the mid-1930s, the Nazi Party came to power in Dietrich's home country of Germany. Led by Adolf Hitler, the Nazis persecuted Jews and other minority groups and made plans for a German takeover

MARLENE DIETRICH, shown here in 1935, received an Oscar nomination for *Morocco*.

of Europe. In the late 1930s, Dietrich denounced the Nazis, cut all ties to Germany, and became a U.S. citizen. During World War II, when the United States went to war against Germany, Italy, and Japan, Dietrich entertained U.S. and Allied troops at military bases. After the war, she continued to act in films.

From 1953 to 1975, Dietrich toured the world as a singer. She spent the final years of her life in Paris and died in 1992. She is remembered for infusing a strain of European exoticism into the normally "all-American" movies of the 1930s.

From 1929 to 1949, **THE MARX BROTHERS—*(LEFT TO RIGHT)* ZEPPO, CHICO, GROUCHO, AND HARPO—**made thirteen films.

All Marx Brothers movies featured slapstick comedy, with lots of pokes at the rich and powerful.

A bit more subtle were the "screwball" comedies of the 1930s. These were lighthearted stories filled with fun, romance, and eccentric characters. In *Bringing up Baby* (1938), for instance, Katharine Hepburn plays Susan, a zany heiress with a pet leopard named Baby. Susan and Baby meet straitlaced zoologist David, played by Cary Grant, and proceed to turn his life upside down and inside out. Audiences loved it.

◼ FOOTLIGHT PARADE

On August 16, 1934, the *New York Times* reviewed a new musical called *Dames*. The reviewer noted that "most members of the first-night audience left the theatre humming or whistling 'I Only Have Eyes for You.'" He also declared,

"The black-and-white effects in the 'Dames' [dance] number certainly are as striking as any ever filmed. It is almost unforgivable to say that the audience gasped. However, 'the audience gasped.'"

It's no surprise that both the audience and the *New York Times* reviewer loved—even gasped at—*Dames*. It was one of a string of 1930s musical extravaganzas by director-choreographer Busby Berkeley. In *Dames, Gold Diggers of 1933, Gold Diggers of 1935, 42nd Street*, and other films, Berkeley wowed audiences with his out-of-this-world dance numbers.

The typical dance scene started with a singer (generally Dick Powell) crooning to his girlfriend (usually Ruby Keeler). Then the camera would pull back to a fantasy set of beautiful and elaborately dressed dancers—usually all women. The dancers would swirl, circle, march, and climb stairs in formation. Berkeley often filmed them from above, turning their dance routines into unique geometric and

BUSBY BERKELEY *(seated at front)* created large dreamlike dance numbers with dozens of dancers for his movies.

kaleidoscopic images. Props such as moving stairways, swirling pianos, waterfalls, and bubble baths added to the fantastical dream world. When it was all over, Dick Powell would be back singing sweetly to Ruby Keeler, as if nothing had ever happened.

It was hard to top Busby Berkeley for dance scenes, but Fred Astaire and Ginger Rogers managed to pull it off. The famous dance partners were symbols of art deco elegance. With Fred in a tuxedo and Ginger in a flowing gown, they danced their way through nine hit films, including *The Gay Divorcée* (1934, with music by Cole Porter), *Top Hat* (1935), and *Swing Time* (1936).

Ginger Rogers and Fred Astaire dance in the film **SWING TIME** in 1936.

◼ KIDDIE FARE

Children made up a big part of the moviegoing audience in the 1930s. Strict censorship rules, especially after 1934, ensured that all movies were family friendly (that is, not too sexually suggestive). Westerns, musicals, and comedies attracted moviegoers of all ages. Still, some movies appealed mostly to kids. If a movie featured a youngster in a leading role (such as Jackie Coogan in *Tom Sawyer* or Jackie Cooper in *Treasure Island*), chances are there would be lots of kids in the audience.

When six-year-old Shirley Temple danced, sang, and charmed her way through *Stand up and Cheer* in 1934, Fox studio heads knew they had a star on their hands. The delightfully dimpled and curly-headed Shirley brought new meaning to the word *cute.* She acted in twenty-two films in the 1930s, including such hits as *Heidi* (1937) and *Rebecca of Sunnybrook*

SHIRLEY TEMPLE charmed audiences during the 1930s.

Farm (1938). Meanwhile, the "Shirley Temple look"—featuring hair bows and ringlets—swept the nation. The Sears, Roebuck mail-order catalog offered "a complete Shirley Temple wardrobe for the little miss." And Shirley was the second most popular name for girls born in 1935 and 1936 (Mary was first).

Kids loved cartoon shorts—so why not make a full-length cartoon movie? Filmmaker Walt Disney did just that with the creation of *Snow White and*

When six-year-old Shirley Temple danced, sang, and charmed her way through *Stand up and Cheer* in 1934, Fox studio heads knew they had a star on their hands.

the Seven Dwarfs (1937), the first-ever feature-length cartoon. To create such a movie in the 1930s (long before computer-generated animation), illustrators had to paint all the pictures by hand. The work was painstaking, requiring more than forty animators and taking three years to complete. The final result was worth all the trouble. *Snow White* was a huge success and even won a special Academy Award. In addition to the brilliant animation, the movie featured terrific songs, including "Whistle While You Work" and "Some Day My Prince Will Come."

■ BAD GUYS

The 1930s saw a number of frightful characters hit the silver screen. Universal Pictures released *Frankenstein* in 1931, with Boris Karloff playing the scary but misunderstood monster. *Bride of Frankenstein* followed in 1935. After playing the lead role in *Dracula* (1931), Bela Lugosi went on to portray additional creepy characters, including zombies, murderers, and mad scientists.

Like Frankenstein, the star of *King Kong* (1933) was sadly misunderstood. Kong, a giant gorilla, could be ferocious, but he

KING KONG dangles Ann Darrow (played by Fay Wray) over New York City.

JAMES CAGNEY was the classic movie mobster of the 1930s.

showed his softer side when he fell in love with a pretty young actress named Ann Darrow (played by Fay Wray). In the movie's dramatic final scene, Kong carries Ann to the top of the Empire State Building. There, fighter pilots assail him with machine gun fire. Kong finally falls to his death. The exciting film won rave reviews for its special effects, and Kong went on to star in many more movies.

The real-life bad guys of the early 1930s were gangsters such as Al Capone. Capone made a fortune selling bootlegged (illegal) liquor—and racked up quite a few murders in the process. The gangsters of the 1930s lived in a shadowy underworld. It was dark, gritty, and dangerous—and just right for the movies. The most famous 1930s gangster movie was *The Public Enemy* (1931), starring James Cagney as the mobster Tom Powers. *Scarface* (1932) starred Paul Muni, who played an Al Capone-like character. *G-Men* (1935) again featured James Cagney, but this time, he helps the good guys—FBI agents trying to put mobsters out of business.

■ "LULLABY OF BROADWAY"

Live theater thrived during the 1930s. The great playwrights of the twentieth century—Eugene O'Neill, Clifford Odets, Lillian Hellman, and Thornton Wilder—produced some of their finest works during the decade. Many of their plays were wrenching dramas that explored political, social, and family struggles.

George Kaufman wrote both plays and musical comedies—usually in collaboration with other writers. He and Edna Ferber penned *Dinner at Eight* (1932) and *Stage Door* (1936), among other comic plays. His collaborations with Moss

Hart included *You Can't Take It with You* (1936) and *The Man Who Came to Dinner* (1939). He teamed with writer Morrie Ryskind and composers George and Ira Gershwin on several musicals, including *Strike Up the Band* (1930). All these shows were later made into movies.

The Gershwin brothers were a top songwriting team. George wrote the music, and Ira wrote the words. Along with writer DuBose Heyward, they created *Porgy and Bess* (1935), a groundbreaking folk opera with an all-black cast. The opera explores life on Catfish Row, a tenement street in Charleston, South Carolina. The show's innovative musical numbers combined jazz, gospel, blues, pop, and opera and included the hit songs "Summertime," "It Ain't Necessarily So," and "I Got Plenty o' Nuttin'."

Anything Goes, with music by Cole Porter, was a smash when it opened on Broadway in 1934. The action takes place on an ocean liner headed for Great Britain. The story offers a clever combination of love, mistaken identity, and high jinks, but the real attraction is Porter's brilliant songs, such as "I Get a Kick out of You," "You're the Top," "It's De-Lovely," and the title number "Anything Goes"—all of which became instant classics.

Ethel Merman, shown here in a publicity still for Cole Porter's ***ANYTHING GOES***, played Reno Sweeney when the show opened on Broadway in 1934.

■ PEOPLE'S THEATER

Even the federal government got into the theater business during the 1930s. The Federal Theater Project (FTP) was yet another division of the Federal Project Number One arts program. The FTP employed out-of-work actors, stagehands, playwrights, set designers, and other theater professionals. Like the Federal Art Project, its goal was not just to give jobs to creative artists but also to bring culture to the U.S. public.

The FTP established theaters in twelve U.S. cities. It staged performances in each city and also set up traveling companies to take the shows on tour. In addition, the FTP gave money to existing local theater groups, created special children's theaters, and created the Federal Theatre of the Air, which staged radio plays.

Members of the **WPA FEDERAL THEATER PROJECT** rehearse *Treasure Island* before launching a summer tour through New York City parks and playgrounds in 1938.

The Federal Theater Project's goal was not just to give jobs to creative artists but also to bring culture to the U.S. public.

In several cities, the FTP put on shows with all-black casts. *The Swing Mikado,* for instance, was a jazzy adaption of *The Mikado,* a famous British operetta (comic opera). The show, staged by an FTP "Negro unit," ran in Chicago for five months. In Harlem in New York City, another "Negro unit" offered a new take on Shakespeare's famous tragedy *Macbeth.* The producers moved the story from Scotland in the eleventh century to Haiti in the nineteenth century. Whereas Shakespeare's original story had involved witchcraft, the Harlem version of *Macbeth* involved voodoo, the magical religion of Haiti.

Several FTP projects were overtly political. For instance, the Living Newspaper series was designed to educate audiences about current affairs. In shows such as *Triple-A Plowed Under, Injunction Granted, Power,* and *One-Third of a Nation* performers acted out scenes from the headlines: labor and farm struggles, unemployment, New Deal programs, and other timely topics. Some members of Congress fumed that the FTP, like the FAP, had been taken over by Communists and radicals.

Despite some criticism, the FTP ran for four years and put on almost

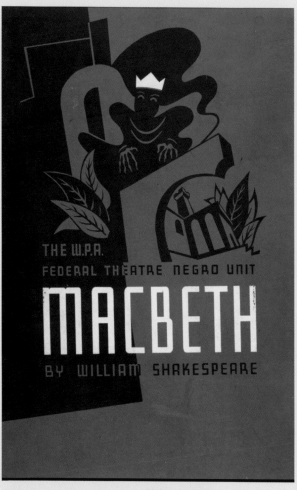

This poster advertised the **FTP "NEGRO UNIT" PRODUCTION OF *MACBETH*.**

sixty-four thousand performances in all. Many soon-to-be-famous actors (Will Geer, Joseph Cotton, and Burt Lancaster) and playwrights (Arthur Miller) found work with the FTP.

■ GOLDEN AGE

The 1930s has been called the golden age of radio. Between 1929 and 1939, the number of U.S. homes equipped with radios rose from about 12 million to 28 million. By 1939 the average family spent four and a half hours every day listening to various programs.

During the daytime, stations mostly broadcast melodramas. These shows were broken into fifteen-minute installments, with commercials for soap and other products in between. It was the advertisements that gave the serials their name—soap operas. By the time the children got home from school, the

A family gathers around the table **TO LISTEN TO THE RADIO** in 1933. The radio components sat inside a big wooden cabinet.

> **"I can hardly force myself to keep looking at it. The eyes are black and gleam like a serpent. The mouth is V-shaped with saliva dripping from its rimless lips that seem to quiver and pulsate."**
>
> —*Orson Welles, describing a Martian in his 1938 "The War of the Worlds" radio broadcast*

morning soap operas had given way to afternoon serials popular with youngsters. These included *The Lone Ranger, Little Orphan Annie,* and *The Green Hornet.* The evening news came on at dinnertime.

After dinner, families gathered around the radio to hear sports, comedies, dramas, and classical music. Variety shows, which featured a mixture of jokes, skits, and popular music, were very popular. *The Chase and Sanborn Hour* (featuring ventriloquist Edgar Bergen and his dummy Charlie McCarthy), *The Jack Benny Show*, and *The Kate Smith Hour* were some of the decade's most well-loved variety shows.

One wildly popular comedy show was *Amos 'n' Andy.* The lead characters were African Americans: the cabdriver Amos, his dim-witted friend Andy, the troublemaking Kingfish, and others. White actors read the lines, using exaggerated accents that mimicked African American dialect. In later decades, civil rights groups criticized *Amos 'n' Andy* for promoting racial stereotypes. The show had few critics in the 1930s, when racism was woven tightly into the fabric of everyday American life.

Edgar Bergen *(center)* poses with his dummies— **CHARLIE MCCARTHY *(LEFT)* AND MORTIMER SNERD**—in 1938.

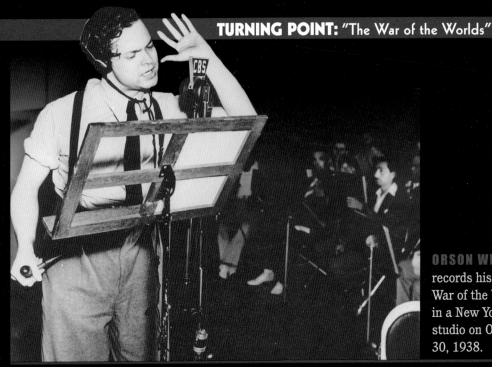

ORSON WELLES records his "The War of the Worlds" in a New York studio on October 30, 1938.

Orson Welles, a young actor-director, hosted a weekly CBS radio show called *Mercury Theatre on the Air*. On October 30, 1938, Welles and his troupe performed a radio play called "The War of the Worlds." The program started out like a typical 1930s music program. It began with dance music from Ramón Raquello and his orchestra.

Suddenly an announcer (Orson Welles) interrupted with a news flash about repeated explosions on the planet Mars. Another bulletin said that a meteorite had landed in New Jersey. A later bulletin said that a group of leather-headed Martians, as tall as skyscrapers, had emerged from the meteorite. Yet another report said that Martians had laid waste to cities in New Jersey and were wading across the Hudson River to New York City.

At several points during the broadcast, an announcer reminded listeners that the show was only fictional, but many listeners, having tuned in from other stations, missed the announcements. Believing the invasion to be real, some listeners panicked. They called the police, grabbed firearms to protect themselves from Martians, or got into their cars and fled.

At the end of the show, Orson Welles chuckled and told listeners, "If your doorbell rings and nobody's there, that was no Martian. It's Halloween." The prank made national headlines. Although the panic had not been widespread (newspapers exaggerated it greatly), Welles and CBS apologized for the trouble they had caused.

Actor Fred Astaire *(left)* sits with composer GEORGE GERSHWIN *(center)* and lyricist IRA GERSHWIN on the set of *Shall We Dance* in 1937.

CHAPTER NINE

LIFE IS JUST A BOWL OF CHERRIES:

MUSIC OF THE 1930s

Edgar "Yip" Harburg faced an uncertain future. It was 1930. The stock market had just crashed. Harburg's electrical appliance business had gone broke. He was thousands of dollars in debt, with a wife and two children to support. How would they survive?

Harburg had a good friend named Ira Gershwin. Already successful as a lyricist (with his brother George), Gershwin suggested that Harburg get into his line of work. A clever writer, Harburg took his friend's advice. He discovered that he loved writing songs and poetry a lot more than selling electrical appliances. He teamed with a composer named Jay Gorney. Together, they began writing songs for Broadway shows.

One of their first shows was called *Americana*. In one scene, men stand in a breadline, waiting for food. The song that Harburg and Gorney wrote for that scene, "Brother, Can You Spare a Dime?" precisely captured the agony of the unemployed. The singer laments that he once built the nation's great skyscrapers and fought heroically in World War I. But by the early thirties, he's been reduced to asking for a handout—a dime for a cup of coffee.

"Brother, Can You Spare a Dime?" became a theme song for the Great Depression. It played everywhere—on records, on the radio, and at live shows. It was a sad song—appropriate for a wearied, worried people—but as Harburg later explained, the message didn't reduce the singer to a beggar. "It makes him a dignified human, asking questions—and a bit outraged, too, as he should be."

"WE'RE IN THE MONEY"

As good as the song was, by the 1932 election, people had had enough of "Brother, Can You Spare a Dime?" It was time for more upbeat songs. FDR's campaign song, "Happy Days Are Here Again," put forward a more positive message. So did "Life Is Just a Bowl of Cherries." "We're in the Money,"

sung by Ginger Rogers (decked out in a costume made of giant gold coins) in *Gold Diggers of 1933*, was perhaps a little too optimistic. After all, the nation was still in the vice grip of the Great Depression, but Americans were by then determined to look on the bright side. Songwriters gave them reasons to smile, with dreamy love songs, rousing show tunes, and jazz instrumentals.

It was an era of great songs: "Ain't Misbehavin'," "I Got Rhythm," "It's Only a Paper Moon," "Stormy Weather," "Blue Moon," "I'm in the Mood for Love," "Lullaby of Broadway," and "Pennies from Heaven"—to name just a few. It was an era of great singers: Fats Waller, Bing Crosby, Rudy Vallee, Bessie Smith, Ethel Waters, Ella Fitzgerald, Billie Holiday, and Ethel Merman—among many. It was an era of great songwriters and songwriting teams: George and Ira Gershwin, Cole Porter, Harold Arlen, Richard Rodgers and Lorenz Hart, Harry Warren and Al Dubin, Jerome Kern, Johnny Mercer—and the list goes on. Many hit songs were written for Broadway shows or movie musicals and then recorded again and again by popular singers.

The federal government recognized the value of music in people's lives and launched the Federal Music Project (FMP) as part of Federal Project Number One in 1935. Headed by Nikolai Sokoloff, former conductor of the Cleveland Orchestra, the FMP created symphony orchestras in dozens of cities, as well as string quartets, military bands, dance bands, choral groups, and opera companies. These groups, usually staffed by highly accomplished musicians, gave regular performances, while audience members paid a small fee (ten to fifty-five cents) to hear the concerts.

The FMP also funded music libraries, music classes, and recordings, and collaborated with the Federal Writers Project to compile folk song collections. As with the other New Deal art projects, the goal was to give jobs to out-of-work musicians, as well as to offer cultural enrichment to the public. When the program ended in 1943, many of the symphonic groups kept going without government funding.

■ SWING!

One cold day in March 1937, thousands of teenagers poured into New York City's huge Paramount Theater. As the show opened, a band on an elevated platform rose out of the orchestra pit. The band was Benny Goodman's, and the music was swing. Many of the young people in the audience screamed. Some began to dance in the aisles.

By then the United States had caught swing fever. Actually, swing was nothing more than jazz under a new name. Spearheaded by "King of Swing" Goodman (a clarinetist as well as a bandleader), swing music featured big bands

BENNY GOODMAN and his orchestra perform at the Roseland Ballroom in New York City in 1938.

of brass, woodwind, and rhythm players. Besides Goodman, great swing bandleaders of the 1930s include Tommy Dorsey, Count Basie, Glenn Miller, Harry James, and Duke Ellington. The bands performed instrumental numbers such as "Begin the Beguine," "Mood Indigo," and "Take the 'A' Train." They also featured vocalists, usually women. Among the chief band singers of the 1930s were Martha Tilton, Helen O'Connell, Billie Holiday, Marion Hutton, and Ella Fitzgerald.

The 1930s swing bands were notable for more than just their music. They

"A name that is world famous . . . Here you will find an exuberant, and exultant, a frenzied gaiety as the merry dancers go 'Stompin' at the Savoy' or 'Lindy Hoppin.'"

—1939 World's Fair brochure, describing Harlem's famous nightclubs

were integrated during an era when most of the nation was segregated. Black and white instrumentalists traveled and played together. Many of the top band singers (Ella Fitzgerald, Lena Horne, and Billie Holiday) were black, as were bandleaders Duke Ellington and Cab Calloway.

Swing bands played at theaters and clubs in New York and other big cities. They also toured smaller towns. Those who couldn't catch a live performance could hear plenty of swing on jukeboxes (introduced in the early 1930s), records, and radio. On Saturday nights, radio's *Your Hit Parade* counted down the top ten songs of the week.

ELLA FITZGERALD
sings with Chick Webb's band in 1938.

In the early decades of the twentieth century, even music was segregated. The big record companies produced a separate line of "race records"—recordings by African American artists—generally blues, jazz, and gospel music, which they marketed to black buyers. Most radio stations wouldn't play music by black artists. But in the late 1920s and early 1930s, the color line in music began to fall. Several black artists earned nationwide fame. One of them was Cab Calloway.

CAB CALLOWAY *(in front of piano)* performs with his orchestra in 1937.

Cabell Calloway III was born on December 25, 1907, in Rochester, New York. His family moved to Baltimore when he was six. In the early 1920s, Calloway enrolled in Crane College in Chicago. His parents wanted him to become a lawyer like his father. He wanted to become an entertainer.

In 1925 his sister helped him land a singing part in *Plantation Days,* an all–African American stage show in Chicago. When the show closed, Calloway dropped out of college and took up singing full-time. He became the emcee (master of ceremonies) for a band called the Alabamians. As the emcee, he conducted the band, introduced the other musicians, sang, told jokes, and generally hammed it up. The Alabamians didn't hit it big, but Calloway's next band,

the Missourians, did. Renamed Cab Calloway and His Orchestra, the group landed a job at the famous Cotton Club in New York City.

Onstage at the Cotton Club, Calloway always dressed in a white silk suit, a top hat, and tails. He became famous for scat singing—that is, inserting nonsense syllables (such as *hi-de-ho* and *skee-tee-tuh-bee*) into his song lyrics. In 1931 he recorded his first big hit, "Minnie the Moocher," which became his theme song.

By 1932 Calloway had made the big time. He and his band performed on radio, cut records, and appeared in Hollywood films. The band stayed on top for the rest of the 1930s and most of the 1940s. They disbanded in 1948.

In the following decades, Calloway performed in a variety of venues. He appeared in Broadway shows, toured with a sextet, and performed as a solo singer. Calloway died in 1994.

Some of the most memorable songs of the 1930s were not swing or scat. They were the honest, simple songs of Woody Guthrie. Guthrie wrote songs about dust bowl migrants, union men and women, and other hardworking people.

Guthrie was born in Okemah, Oklahoma, in 1912. During his boyhood, he loved singing, drawing, and playing the harmonica. But times were hard. His family suffered through a series of tragic events: the death of his older sister, his father's financial ruin, and his mother's severe illness that later took her life.

In 1931 Guthrie moved to Pampa, Texas, where he married and started a family. By this time, he had learned to play the guitar. He and two friends started an old-time country band, the Corn Cob Trio.

When dust storms hit Texas, Guthrie left his family and traveled west. He rode freight trains, hitchhiked, and walked. When he got to California, he landed a job singing on the radio. He also got involved in politics. He sang at union meetings and Communist Party rallies. During this period, Guthrie wrote songs about the dust bowl, including "Talking Dust Bowl Blues," "Dust Bowl Refugees," and "Tom Joad" (based on John Steinbeck's *The Grapes of Wrath*).

In 1940 Guthrie moved east to New York City. There, the folk music community embraced him as an authentic American voice. He made recordings for the Library of Congress, joined a band called the Alma-

WOODY GUTHRIE described the struggles and pride of Americans in his Depression-era songs.

nac Singers, and performed on the radio. Guthrie spent the rest of the 1940s traveling, writing songs, and performing.

In the 1950s, although he continued to sing and write songs, Guthrie's behavior became more and more unusual. He was finally diagnosed with Huntington's chorea, the hereditary disease that had killed his mother. The disease destroyed Guthrie's central nervous system. Eventually, he could no longer care for himself and had to be hospitalized.

Guthrie died in 1967. By then he had become a folk music legend. His musical legacy encompasses more than one thousand songs, including the famous "This Land Is Your Land."

■ "TEN CENTS A DANCE"

Dance ran the gamut in the 1930s—from a small-town Saturday night pastime to big-budget entertainment. Ordinary Americans danced at local nightclubs, high school gyms, and social halls. Some venues hired local dance bands to play live music. If there was no band, a jukebox stacked with records did the job. When the music started, young people jumped up to do the jitterbug and other swing dances.

At movie houses, viewers could see professional dancers at the top of their games. Tap dancer Bill "Bojangles" Robinson made four movies with Shirley Temple in the 1930s. (Robinson was an African American and usually relegated to playing the part of a butler or other servant.) Broadway shows always featured brilliant dance numbers along with the singing and comedy.

The Martha Graham Dance Company didn't go in for typical song-and-dance routines. In 1931 Graham's troupe staged a work called *Primitive Mysteries.* This piece, based on traditional Native American religion, was unlike anything seen before. The dancers (all women) made jerking movements. They struck angular poses. With her "modern dance," Graham attempted to explore difficult human emotions. At first, audiences and critics scratched their heads, but eventually Graham attracted a strong following. Far more traditional in his approach to dance, George Balanchine founded the School of American Ballet in New York City in 1934.

A young couple **DANCES THE JITTERBUG** in the late 1930s.

The New York Giants play the Washington Senators in the 1933
WORLD SERIES. Baseball was a very popular pastime in the 1930s.

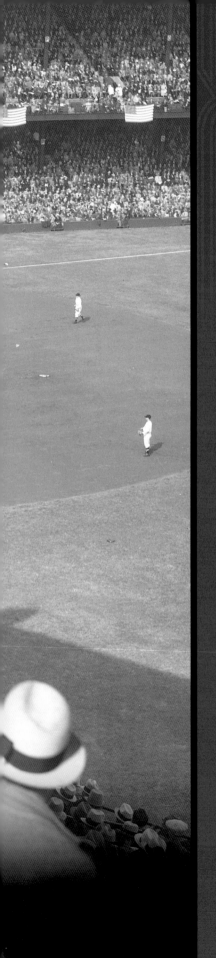

CHAPTER TEN

"TAKE ME OUT TO THE BALL GAME":

SPORTS OF THE 1930s

In the 1930s, a ticket to a baseball game cost about fifty cents. That was no small change in an era when the typical worker earned less than five dollars a day. Not surprisingly, as the Depression deepened, many fans stopped coming to games. Many minor-league teams went out of business early in the decade.

The major leagues adjusted—cutting players' salaries and holding night games to attract more fans. The first All-Star game (the best players from the National League versus the best from the American League) took place in Chicago in 1933. In 1936 a committee of baseball executives created the Baseball Hall of Fame and named the first five inductees: Babe Ruth, Ty Cobb, Honus Wagner, Christy Mathewson, and Walter Johnson. A building to house the organization, the National Baseball Hall of Fame and Museum, opened in Cooperstown, New York, in 1939.

Despite financial woes, the 1930s were something of a golden era for baseball. No one had ever seen a team quite like the 1934 Saint Louis Cardinals. Sportswriters called them the Gashouse Gang because they were rough and rowdy—like workers from the city's gasworks district. They had some powerful hitters, but their greatest strength came from two pitchers, brothers Jerome "Dizzy" and

JEROME "DIZZY" (LEFT) AND PAUL "DAFFY" DEAN were two of the best pitchers in professional baseball in the 1930s.

Paul "Daffy" Dean. In 1934 Dizzy won thirty games and Daffy won nineteen. The brothers then pitched their team to victory in the World Series against the Detroit Tigers.

As good as the Cardinals were, the New York Yankees were even better. Led by Lou Gehrig, Joe DiMaggio, and others, the team racked up five World Series wins in the 1930s. Home run king Babe Ruth—perhaps the greatest slugger of all time—left the Yankees in 1934 and retired from baseball altogether in 1935.

In the world of football, the college game was more popular than the pros in the 1930s. Michigan and Ohio State were fierce rivals,

as were Army and Navy, Auburn and Georgia, Notre Dame and the University of Southern California, and Pittsburgh and Penn State. Famous college bowl games—the Orange, Sugar, and Cotton—all debuted in the 1930s. In 1935 the Downtown Athletic Club in New York awarded the first Heisman Trophy to the top college football player. The winner was Jay Berwanger, a halfback for the University of Chicago.

"I consider myself the luckiest man on the face of the earth. I have been in ballparks for 17 years, and I have never received anything but kindness and encouragement from you fans."

—New York Yankee Lou Gehrig, bidding farewell to fans after his diagnosis with amyotrophic lateral sclerosis (later called Lou Gehrig's disease), 1939

Professional sports were segregated in the 1930s. Big-league baseball teams hired only white players. Blacks were shunted into the Negro Leagues—where even the greatest baseball players of all time earned little notice and low pay. National football and basketball leagues were also all white. Independent of any organized league, the all-black Harlem Globetrotters basketball team (formed in 1926) traveled from town to town, drumming up local opponents and consistently beating all of them.

■ FAIRWAYS

Golf was a rich man's game in the 1930s. At exclusive country clubs, players dressed in knickers (knee-length pants) and natty caps knocked around balls for fun. Later, over drinks at the clubhouse, they talked business. On the professional golf circuit, athletes such as Sam Snead and Ben Hogan played for cash prizes.

Golf might have been a rich *man's* game—but that didn't keep teenage Patty Berg off the fairways. In 1934, when Berg was just fourteen, her father bought her a secondhand set of golf clubs. One year later, she won the Minneapolis, Minnesota, city championship. During the next seven years, she won seven women's titles, including the prestigious U.S. Women's Amateur in 1938.

Thousands of people crowd into Yankee Stadium to see **ARMY (THE U.S. MILITARY ACADEMY) PLAY NOTRE DAME** in 1933.

Satchel Paige was one of the greatest pitchers in baseball history. Unfortunately for fans—and for Paige himself—not many people knew about his greatness during his playing days.

LeRoy Robert Paige was born about 1906 in Mobile, Alabama. As a boy, he earned a little money by toting satchels, or bags, for passengers at the Mobile railroad station. That job earned him the nickname Satchel.

Paige learned to pitch a baseball at the Industrial School for Negro Children in Mount Meigs, Alabama. After leaving school in 1923, he joined a semipro, all-black baseball team, the Mobile Tigers. He moved up to the professional Negro Leagues in 1926 when he joined the Chattanooga Black Lookouts.

Paige played with various Negro League teams before settling in with the Pittsburgh Crawfords in 1932. With Paige on the mound, the Crawfords dominated the league. In the late 1930s, Paige played baseball in Mexico for a brief period. He joined the Kansas City Monarchs in 1939.

Paige's brilliant pitching earned him the admiration of fans and fellow players. He occasionally pitched in exhibition games against big-league white players. After facing him on several occasions, Joe DiMaggio declared that Paige was the greatest pitcher in baseball. Despite his talents, Paige was not allowed to officially compete

SATCHEL PAIGE led the Kansas City Monarchs to a Negro World Series Championship in 1942.

against DiMaggio and other big leaguers. The major leagues remained segregated until 1947.

Paige finally joined a major-league team, the Cleveland Indians, in 1948. Although past his prime, he did good work for Cleveland and later for the Saint Louis Browns. In the late twentieth century, the baseball world finally acknowledged the achievements and contributions of Paige and the other Negro Leaguers. In 1971 Paige was inducted into the National Baseball Hall of Fame.

Berg's rival on the golf course was the superathelete Mildred "Babe" Didrikson. She could drive a golf ball more than 250 yards (229 m)—farther than many male players can drive a golf ball. She often outdistanced her opponents by 150 yards (137 m). She entered her first golf tournament in 1934, winning first place with a score of 77. Didrikson and Berg dominated women's golf for the next two decades.

■ "FOR THE GLORY OF SPORT"

The United States snared both Olympic contests in 1932. The Winter Games took place in Lake Placid, New York, while the Summer Games were in Los Angeles.

BABE DIDRIKSON tees off during a tournament in California in 1936.

At Lake Placid, Norwegian ice skater Sonja Henie glided to an easy gold medal. Recognizing a star when they saw one, Twentieth Century Fox quickly rushed Henie to Hollywood and put her in the movies (where she always played a figure skater). In Los Angeles, Babe Didrikson (in her pregolf career) won gold medals in javelin and hurdles and a silver medal in the high jump. Meanwhile, U.S. swimmer Eleanor Holm captured a gold medal in the 100-meter backstroke. Like Henie, she then transitioned from sports to show business. She starred in the 1938 film *Tarzan's Revenge* and headlined the Aquacades, a popular water show at the 1939 World's Fair.

The 1936 Olympics took place in Berlin, Germany. By this time, Nazi dictator Adolf Hitler had taken control of Germany. Hitler viewed the Olympic contests as an opportunity to prove that white, northern Europeans were physically superior to people of other races.

Enter African American Jesse Owens—the grandson of slaves and the most dominant track star in the United States. At the Berlin Games, Owens held

JESSE OWENS
(center) salutes during the presentation of his gold medal for the long jump at the 1936 Olympics in Germany. Silver medalist Luz Long *(right)* gives the Nazi salute.

off teammate Ralph Metcalfe to claim the gold medal in the 100-meter sprint. Then he breezed to an easy win in the 200 meters. In the long jump, he defeated Germany's Luz Long to gain his third gold medal. Owens's fourth victory came in the 4-by-100 relay.

According to legend, Hitler was incensed and pointedly refused to congratulate Owens after his victory. In fact, except for the first day of competition, Hitler didn't congratulate any of the Olympic victors. The more than one hundred thousand spectators in the stadium, however, showered Owens with applause.

■ A DAY AT THE RACES

Horse racing attracted fans by the millions in the 1930s. Many men (and occasionally women) went to the track to bet on horses, while others listened to races announced on the radio. The decade saw three Triple Crown winners (those who won the Kentucky Derby, Preakness Stakes, and Belmont Stakes all in one season): Gallant Fox in 1930, Omaha in 1935, and War Admiral in 1937.

JOE LOUIS *(left)* watches Max Schmeling fall in the first round of their 1938 match at Yankee Stadium in New York.

Boxing was wildly popular with Americans in the early twentieth century. One of the sport's greatest talents, Joe Louis, dominated the ring in the 1930s. Louis was an African American—nicknamed the Brown Bomber by the press and a hero to other black Americans.

As an amateur in the 1920s and early 1930s, Louis won fifty of fifty-four bouts. In the summer of 1934, he turned pro, and by the fall of 1935, he had defeated twenty-six opponents. On June 22, 1937, Louis defeated James Braddock to become the heavyweight champion of the world.

The new world champion had a huge grudge to settle. In 1936 German boxer Max Schmeling had knocked him out in the twelfth round. Schmeling had studied films of Louis's previous bouts and had detected a flaw in his defenses. Louis tended to drop his left arm whenever he threw a hard right, making him vulnerable to Schmeling's right

cross. In the 1936 fight, Schmeling had belted Louis repeatedly with right-hand punches before putting him down for the count.

A rematch was scheduled for the night of June 22, 1938. Louis camouflaged a burning desire for revenge under his usual placid expression. When the bell clanged, Louis struck with power-laden fists. He floored Schmeling three times before the referee halted the one-sided affair two minutes into the first round.

Louis's victory resonated beyond the world of sports. By 1938 Nazi Germany was threatening its neighbors in Europe and relations between the United States and Germany had grown tense. Because Schmeling was German, many Americans branded him a Nazi. They saw the Louis-Schmeling fight as a triumph of U.S. democracy over German dictatorship. The Germans, for their part, convinced of their own racial superiority, were humiliated by Schmeling's loss to a black man.

In 1938 racing fans went wild for an undersized, crooked-legged racehorse named Seabiscuit. His appearances set attendance records at nearly every major track in the United States. Seabiscuit didn't win all the races he entered, but running against the nation's best horses, he shattered more than one dozen track records.

The Pimlico Special was a much-anticipated showdown between Seabiscuit and Triple Crown winner War Admiral in 1938. For the millions of race fans listening on the radio, an announcer relayed the excitement:

> This is a real horserace—just what we hoped we'd get. They're head and head, and both jockeys driving. It's the best horse from here in. They've got 200 yards [183 m] to come. It's horse against horse. Both of 'em driving. Seabiscuit leads by a length. Now Seabiscuit by a length and a half. . . . Seabiscuit by three. Seabiscuit by three. Seabiscuit is the winner by four lengths. And you never saw such a wild crowd . . . they're roaring around me.

SEABISCUIT edges out **WAR ADMIRAL** at the Pimlico racetrack in Maryland in 1938.

■ FUN AND GAMES

Of course, athletics were not limited to the pros in the 1930s. Kids swam, played ball, and rode bikes after school. High schools and colleges had organized sports teams. Many adults unwound at the neighborhood bowling alley after work and on weekends.

Few working-class people played golf in the 1930s. The greens fees were too high for cash-strapped Americans. A cheaper alternative was miniature golf, which soared in popularity soon after the stock market crash. By 1930 the United States had an estimated thirty thousand miniature golf courses. The mini golf craze even led to a number of popular songs, such as "I'm Put-Put-Puttin' on the Dinky Links All Day" (1930).

For those who were less athletic, billiards, bingo, card games, and board games passed the time. Especially in rural areas, men liked to hunt and fish. And in a decade when the automobile was a fairly new invention, the Sunday drive in the country was an exhilarating pastime—especially in a roadster, or convertible.

The first drive-in movie theater opened in Camden, New Jersey, in 1933. With this development, Americans could combine two of their favorite activities: motoring and moviegoing.

123

ADOLF HITLER'S RISE TO POWER IN GERMANY worried many Americans in the 1930s.

GONE WITH THE WIND

The 1930s wound down, but the Depression did not. By the end of the decade, the nation's unemployment rate stood at 15 percent. That figure was an improvement over the worst unemployment numbers—almost 25 percent out of work in 1933—but it still represented an economic crisis. The New Deal had lessened the impact of the Depression, but it hadn't fixed the economy.

Americans had been focused on their own problems for most of the decade. They didn't care much to look outward—to troubles brewing in Europe and Asia. But they didn't have a choice. By the 1930s, Adolf Hitler, leader of the Nazi Party, had taken over in Germany. Benito Mussolini, head of the National Fascist Party, controlled Italy. Both men ruled as dictators—leaders with absolute power. Both espoused Fascism, a system of government control over all political, economic, and cultural activities in a nation.

Americans watched nervously as Hitler drew more and more power into his own hands. His government became increasingly repressive, particularly toward German Jews. A series of laws barred Jews from certain occupations and stripped them of their property and their German citizenship. In Italy Mussolini took control of industry, schools, the press, and the police. Noam Chomsky, a U.S. scholar

and political activist, recalls how Americans worried as the European dictators grew more aggressive:

> There was at that time a sense of foreboding that was quite serious. . . . There was this extremely frightening Fascist cloud spreading over Europe. I can remember as a child listening to Hitler's speeches [in German] over the radio. I didn't understand them, but the emotional tone was unmistakable. You didn't have to understand the words. It was a very frightening period. It wasn't clear what was going to happen.

At the same time, military leaders had taken over in the Asian nation of Japan. Germany, Italy, and Japan all made plans to invade weaker nations in Europe, Africa, and Asia. They also made an alliance, agreeing to support one another's military efforts. As these events unfolded, it seemed likely that Europe would become engulfed in another great war. Adding Japan to the mix, that war promised to become global.

Having sent their sons, brothers, and husbands off to die in Europe in World War I, many Americans wanted no part of another bloody European war. In the late 1930s, Congress passed a series of strongly worded neutrality acts, which forbade the United States to sell or transport arms to warring nations or to loan them money. An organization called America First took the lead in arguing for isolation, or staying out of foreign affairs completely.

■ FROM DEPRESSION TO WAR

By 1939 neutrality and isolation seemed less and less likely for the United States. Germany seized Czechoslovakia in March 1939, and on September 1, 1939, Germany invaded Poland. Two days after the invasion, Great Britain and France declared war on Germany. The United States would no longer remain neutral. It began supplying arms to its British and French allies. It also began gearing up for war.

War officially came to the United States on December 7, 1941, when Japanese planes bombed the U.S. naval base at Pearl Harbor, Hawaii. When war

THE JAPANESE ATTACK ON THE U.S. NAVAL BASE AT PEARL HARBOR, Hawaii, on December 7, 1941, brought the United States into World War II.

arrived, the Depression ended soon after. Factories making weapons and equipment for U.S. soldiers operated around the clock. Businesses were desperate for workers. Anyone who wanted a job could get one, and pay was high. One woman remembered, "When we got married [in the late 1930s], my husband was making $14 a week." Then war arrived, and "from $14 a week, we jumped to $65 a week, working in a defense plant. It sort of went to my head. Wow! Boy, we were rich."

Indeed, the Depression had finally ended, but Americans were facing a new crucible—another world war. It was a high price to pay for prosperity.

■ LOOKING BACKWARD

During the 1940s, people were happy to have the Great Depression behind them. They remembered the 1930s as a time of suffering and deprivation. But in later decades, Americans began to reflect on the enormous effect that the 1930s, the Great Depression, and the New Deal had had on U.S. society.

Even in the twenty-first century, the legacy of the 1930s remains in plain view. Some New Deal agencies—the Social Security Administration, the Securities and Exchange Commission, the Federal Housing Administration, and others—are still part of the social fabric. When retired and disabled Americans receive monthly Social Security checks, they can thank Franklin Roosevelt and the New Deal for creating the program in 1935.

The debates fueled by the New Deal are also still current. Modern politicians regularly consider: How much should government help poor people? How much should government regulate business? When the Republicans and Democrats battle over issues such as the federal minimum wage, they are continuing arguments started in the 1930s. When the U.S. stock market nosedived in October 2008, commentators made many comparisons to the 1929 crash and the Great Depression. They wondered whether it was time for a new New Deal to jump-start the U.S. economy.

THE TRIBOROUGH BRIDGE, later renamed the Robert F. Kennedy Bridge, was built by the PWA in the 1930s. It is still a main thoroughfare in New York City.

The 1930s seem like a long time ago—and they were. But the careful observer can still see reminders of the 1930s in modern life. In a downtown post office, you might see a

The debates fueled by the New Deal are also still current. Modern politicians regularly consider: How much should government help poor people? How much should government regulate business?

Federal Art Project mural. You might someday visit a PWA-built structure, such as the Triborough Bridge (renamed the Robert F. Kennedy Bridge) in New York City, the Department of the Interior Building in Washington, D.C., or the Bonneville Dam in Washington State. Thirties high style lives on in the grand art deco skyscrapers of Manhattan. Modern Americans can rent *Gold Diggers of 1933* for a little Depression-era song and dance. Want to hear Cab Calloway sing "Minnie the Moocher"? You can watch it on YouTube.

What you can't see—and what modern Americans might never be able to understand—is just how frightened and desperate people were during the Great Depression. But in the face of adversity, people still managed to make brilliant music, art, and movies; build big high-tech bridges, power plants, and airplanes; and create a better society. When remembering the 1930s, perhaps it is these achievements—not the pain and suffering—that can remain foremost in the legacy of the era.

1930
- More than twenty-five thousand U.S. businesses go bankrupt.
- Unemployment figures nearly triple over the year before.
- The 3M Company introduces Scotch tape.
- The Chrysler Building is completed.
- Grant Wood creates *American Gothic.*
- Yip Harburg writes "Brother Can You Spare a Dime?"

1931
- Drought hits the Great Plains.
- The nine Scottsboro Boys are tried for rape in Alabama.
- The Empire State Building is completed.
- Universal Pictures releases *Frankenstein.*
- James Cagney stars in *The Public Enemy.*
- Cab Calloway records "Minnie the Moocher."

1932
- Franklin D. Roosevelt is elected president.
- Soldiers attack the Bonus Army encampment in Washington, D.C.
- Amelia Earhart flies alone across the Atlantic Ocean.
- Radio City Music Hall opens in New York.
- Babe Didrikson wins two gold medals and one silver medal at the Summer Olympic Games in Los Angeles, California.

1933
- The New Deal begins.
- The Twenty-first Amendment to the U.S. Constitution ends Prohibition.
- Windstorms hit the Great Plains, starting the dust bowl.
- Franklin Roosevelt gives his first radio Fireside Chat.
- Wiley Post makes the first solo flight around the world.
- RKO Radio Pictures releases *King Kong.*

1934
- Congress creates the Rural Electrification Administration to bring power to farm families.
- The Saint Louis Cardinals, led by Dizzy and Daffy Dean, win the World Series.
- Dell Publishing introduces the first comic book, *Famous Funnies.*
- *Anything Goes* opens on Broadway.
- George Balanchine founds the School of American Ballet.

1935
- Congress passes the Social Security Act.
- Congress establishes the Works Progress Administration.
- Thomas Hart Benton completes a mural called *Social History of the State of Missouri*.
- *Porgy and Bess* opens on Broadway.
- The Downtown Athletic Club awards the first Heisman Trophy.

1936
- Franklin Roosevelt is elected to a second term as president.
- A&P opens its first supermarket.
- Dale Carnegie publishes *How to Win Friends and Influence People*.
- Dorothea Lange takes her "Migrant Mother" photograph.
- Jesse Owens wins four gold medals at the Berlin Olympics.
- Baseball executives create the National Baseball Hall of Fame.

1937
- The Golden Gate Bridge is completed in San Francisco.
- The *Hindenburg* airship explodes upon landing in New Jersey.
- Amelia Earhart, attempting to fly around the world, disappears with her copilot over the Pacific Ocean.
- *Snow White and the Seven Dwarfs* appears in movie theaters.
- Charlie McCarthy (and ventriloquist Edgar Bergen) debuts on radio.

1938
- Kate Smith first sings "God Bless America" on the radio.
- Orson Welles and the Mercury Players perform "The War of the Worlds" Halloween spoof on radio.
- Superman debuts in DC's Action Comics series.
- Boxer Joe Louis knocks out German Max Schmeling.

1939
- World War II begins in Europe.
- Pan American Airways offers the first transatlantic passenger flight.
- Marian Anderson sings at the Lincoln Memorial, in Washington, D.C.
- John Steinbeck publishes *The Grapes of Wrath*.
- *The Wizard of Oz* plays in movie theaters.

5   Robert S. McElvaine, *The Great Depression: America, 1929–1941* (New York: Times Books, 1993), 18.

8   Bryan B. Sterling and Frances N. Sterling, eds., *A Will Rogers Treasury. Reflections and Observations* (New York: Crown Publishers, 1982), 153.

13 Studs Terkel, *Hard Times: An Oral History of the Great Depression* (New York: Pantheon Books, 1970), 30.

14 Ibid., 31.

14 T. H. Watkins, *The Hungry Years: A Narrative History of the Great Depression in America* (New York: Henry Holt and Company, 1999), 42.

15 McElvaine, *Great Depression*, 173.

16 Ibid., 174–175.

17 White House, "Herbert Hoover," *The White House*, 2008, http://www.whitehouse.gov/history/presidents/hh31.html (August 13, 2008).

18 Lorraine Glennon, ed., *Our Times: The Illustrated History of the 20th Century* (Atlanta: Turner Publishing, 1995), 222.

19 Paul F. Boller Jr., *Presidential Campaigns* (New York: Oxford University Press, 1984), 169.

20 Woody Guthrie, *Bound for Glory* (New York: Plume, 1983), 267–268.

20 Watkins, *Hungry Years*, 72.

23 Ibid., 82–83.

24 Ibid., 427.

25 David E. Kyvig, *Daily Life in the United States, 1920–1940: How Americans Lived through the "Roaring Twenties" and the Great Depression* (Chicago: Ivan R. Dee, 2002), 184.

27 James Gregory, *American Exodus: The Dust Bowl Migrants and Okie Culture in California* (New York: Oxford University Press, 1989), 100–101.

27 John Steinbeck, *The Grapes of Wrath* (New York: Penguin, 1992), 259.

29 *International Herald Tribune*, "In Our Pages: 100, 75, and 50 Years Ago,"

May 2, 2005, http://www.iht.com/articles/2005/05/01/news/old2.php (August 13, 2008).

32 Sterling and Sterling, *Will Rogers Treasury*, 216.

32 Ibid.

33 Watkins, *Hungry Years*, 357.

34 NARA, "On the Bank Crisis," *Franklin D. Roosevelt Presidential Library and Museum*, 2008, http://www.fdrlibrary.marist.edu/031233.html (August 13, 2008).

35 Terkel, *Hard Times*, 58.

35 NARA, "On the Bank Crisis."

36–37 McElvaine, *Great Depression*, 115–116.

41 Watkins, *Hungry Years*, 327.

41 Terkel, *Hard Times*, 125.

43 Woody Guthrie, *Woody Sez* (New York: Grosset and Dunlap, 1975), 133.

45 McElvaine, *Great Depression*, 245.

51 Adclassix.com, "1939 Studebaker," *Adclassix.com*, 2008, http://www.adclassix.com/ads2/39studebakersedan.htm (August 13, 2008).

53 Family of Amelia Earhart, "Amelia Earhart: Celebrating 100 Years of Flight," *AmeliaEarhart.com*, 2008, http://www.ameliaearhart.com/about/biography2.html (August 13, 2008).

56 David Gelernter, *1939: The Lost World of the Fair* (New York: Free Press, 1995), 36–37.

57 National Rural Electric Cooperative Association, *The Next Greatest Thing* (Washington, DC: NRECA, 1984), 2.

57 Ibid.

59 Watkins, *Hungry Years*, 366.

60 Ibid., 368.

62 Terkel, *Hard Times*, 82.

64 McElvaine, *Great Depression*, 187.

69 Ibid., 175.

69 Susan Ware, *Holding Their Own: American Women in the 1930s* (Boston: Twayne Publishers, 1982), 1.

72 Bernard A. Weisberger, ed., *The WPA Guide to America: The Best of 1930s*

America as Seen by the Federal Writers Project (New York: Pantheon Books, 1985), 342–343.

73 Ray Walters, "Paperbacks; 1939: The Birth of the Modern Paperback," *New York Times*, April 30, 1989, http://query.nytimes.com/gst/fullpage.html?res=950DE1D61E3CF933A05757C0A96F948260 (August 13, 2008).

73 Simon & Schuster, "Pocket," *SimonSays.com*, 2007, http://www.simonsays.com/content/destination.cfm?tab=1&pid=427726&agid=13 (August 13, 2008).

76 Karen Vanuska, "Review from the Archives: *Gone with the Wind*," *Karen Vanuska*, July 3, 2008, http://karenvanuska.livejournal.com/tag/margaret+mitchell (August 13, 2008).

76 Dale Carnegie Training, "Welcome to Dale Carnegie Prairie Provinces Canada, *Dale Carnegie Training*, 2008, http://www.carnegietraining.ca/ (August 13, 2008).

80 Robert Hughes, *American Visions: The Epic History of Art in America* (New York: Alfred A. Knopf, 1997), 458.

81 Peter Marshall, "Vintage Etiquette and Tradition," *The Black Tie Guide*, 2008, http://www.blacktieguide.com/Vintage/Etiquette.htm (August 13, 2008).

85 Watkins, *Hungry Years*, 275.

86 Library of Congress, "By the People, for the People: Posters from the WPA, 1936–1943," *American Memory*, August 31, 2000, http://memory.loc.gov/ammem/wpaposters/wpahome.html (August 13, 2008).

87 Michelle Anne Delany, "WWII Photographic Perspectives," *Views: The Newsletter of the Visual Materials Section, Society of American Archivists*, December 2006, http://www.lib.lsu.edu/SAA/dec06.pdf (February 20, 2009).

88–89 Library of Congress, "Dorothea Lange's 'Migrant Mother' Photographs in the Farm Security Administration Collection: An Overview," *Library of Congress Prints and Photographs Reading Room*, December 4, 2007, http://www.loc.gov/rr/print/list/128_migm.html (August 13, 2008).

89 Henry Mietkiewicz, "Great Krypton Superman Was the Star's Ace Reporter," *Toronto Star*, April 26, 1992, A10.

94–95 *New York Times*, "Dames (1934) Words and Music," August 16, 1934, http://movies.nytimes.com/movie/review?_r=3&res=9F01E3DA1339E33ABC4E52DFBE66838F629EDE&oref=slogin&oref=slogin&oref=slogin (August 13, 2008).

97 Kyvig, *Daily Life*, 103.

104 Glennon, *Our Times*, 275.

105 Editors of Time-Life Books, *1930s* (New York: Time-Life, 1969), 35.

107 Terkel, *Hard Times*, 21.

110 Gelernter, *1939*, 5.

116 Glennon, *Our Times*, 283.

122 "Seabiscuit vs. War Admiral—1938 Match Race," *YouTube.com*, 2008, http://www.youtube.com/watch?v=WVT2MPNCqgM&feature=related (August 13, 2008).

126 BBC, "The Interview," *BBC Radio World Service*, October 25, 2008, http://www.bbc.co.uk/worldservice/programmes/the_interview.shtml (October 25, 2008).

127 Terkel, *Hard Times*, 95.

SELECTED BIBLIOGRAPHY

Agee, James, and Walker Evans. *Let Us Now Praise Famous Men.* 1941. Reprint, New York: Houghton Mifflin Company, 1980.
In the summer of 1936, journalist James Agee and photographer Walker Evans lived with three sharecropper families in rural Alabama and recorded their lives in words and pictures. This groundbreaking work illuminates the despair and deprivations endured by the poorest Americans during the Great Depression.

Basinger, Jeanine. *The Star Machine.* New York: Alfred A. Knopf, 2007.
From the 1930s to the 1950s, Hollywood studios "manufactured" stars, tightly controlled their media images, and carefully managed their careers. This book explores some of the "products" of the studio system, including 1930s superstars Tyrone Power, Errol Flynn, and William Powell.

Burroughs, Polly. *Thomas Hart Benton: A Portrait.* Garden City, NY: Doubleday and Company, 1981.
During the 1930s, many artists worked in the "regionalist" style. One of the most accomplished was Thomas Hart Benton. His scenes of midwestern life and landscapes have become icons of 1930s America. This book tells Benton's story through words and images.

Gelernter, David. *1939: The Lost World of the Fair.* New York: Free Press, 1995.
The 1939 World's Fair in New York displayed the best of U.S. technology, design, and business to the fair-going public. It also presented a vision of the future. Gelernter uses the fair as a springboard for discussions of late 1930s America.

Glennon, Lorraine, ed. *Our Times: The Illustrated History of the 20th Century.* Atlanta: Turner Publishing, 1995.
This terrific book examines the twentieth century year by year, with coverage of art, politics, sports, and entertainment. Colorful photographs and illustrations bring history to life.

Hughes, Robert. *American Visions: The Epic History of Art in America.* New York: Alfred A. Knopf, 1997.
This brilliant book examines American history by exploring American art and architecture. A chapter called "Streamlines and Breadlines" discusses art trends in the 1920s and 1930s—from the ornate skyscrapers of New York to WPA murals to the futuristic 1939 World's Fair.

Kyvig, David E. *Daily Life in the United States, 1920–1940: How Americans Lived through the "Roaring Twenties" and the Great Depression.* Chicago: Ivan R. Dee, 2002.
In the 1920s, with new conveniences such as radio, cars, and electrical appliances, American life speeded up. In the following decade, the nation fell headfirst into the Great Depression. Kyvig examines how Americans adjusted to changes in society, economy, and daily life in both decades.

McElvaine, Robert S. *The Great Depression: America, 1929–1941.* New York: Times Books, 1993.
McElvaine examines the Depression years from many angles. He explores the roots of the economic disaster, the New Deal, the various social and political movements that emerged during the 1930s, and day-to-day life for ordinary Americans.

National Rural Electric Cooperative Association. *The Next Greatest Thing.* Washington, DC: NRECA, 1984.
In 1934 the U.S. government created the Rural Electrification Administration to bring electrical power to U.S. farmers. On the fiftieth anniversary of this event, the NRECA created this fascinating commemorative book. It tells the story of rural electrification in words and pictures.

Roosevelt, Eleanor. *Eleanor Roosevelt's My Day: Her Acclaimed Columns, 1936–1945.* New York: Pharos Books, 1989.
First Lady Eleanor Roosevelt wrote her My Day newspaper column for twenty-six years. The columns gave ordinary Americans a feeling of personal connection to Roosevelt and her family. This collection includes columns written during the difficult years of the Depression and World War II.

Sterling, Bryan B., and Frances N. Sterling, eds. *A Will Rogers Treasury: Reflections and Observations.* New York: Crown Publishers, 1982.
Will Rogers wrote a daily newspaper column, acted in movies, and gave humorous talks on the stage and radio. Here, the Sterlings highlight some of Rogers's best newspaper writings. These clever observations offer a window into American life in the 1920s and 1930s.

Terkel, Studs. *Hard Times: An Oral History of the Great Depression.* New York: Pantheon Books, 1970.
Acclaimed writer and radio commentator Studs Terkel interviewed dozens of Americans about their experiences in the Great Depression. The interviews are collected in this fascinating and famous book.

Watkins, T. H. *The Hungry Years: A Narrative History of the Great Depression in America.* New York: Henry Holt and Company, 1999.
Watkins examines the Depression years in great detail. He tells the stories of ordinary Americans and how they coped with poverty, fear, and crisis.

Weisberger, Bernard A., ed. *The WPA Guide to America: The Best of 1930s America as Seen by the Federal Writers Project.* New York: Pantheon Books, 1985.
The Federal Writers Project gave jobs to more than six thousand Americans—some of whom went on to become famous authors. The FWP also produced some stellar works, most notably the American Guide Series on U.S. states, regions, and cities. This anthology offers a sampling of that great writing.

Books

Aretha, David. *The Trial of the Scottsboro Boys.* Greensboro, NC: Morgan Reynolds Publishing, 2007.
The U.S. justice system promises everyone a fair trial—but when nine black teenagers went on trial for rape in 1931, fairness was nowhere to be found. This book explores the famous trial and how it helped launch the civil rights movement.

Roberts, Jeremy. *Franklin D. Roosevelt.* Minneapolis: Twenty-First Century Books, 2003.
Franklin Roosevelt had the tough job of leading the United States through both the Great Depression and World War II. At the same time, he struggled with his own physical disability. This book tells his life story.

Coombs, Karen Mueller. *Woody Guthrie: America's Folksinger.* Minneapolis: Twenty-First Century Books, 2002.
Woody Guthrie left the dust bowl in the 1930s with little more than his guitar and the clothes on his back. He found himself caught up in union struggles, New Deal projects, and the East Coast folk music scene. This artful biography captures both Guthrie's brilliance and his flaws.

Cooper, Michael L. *Dust to East: Drought and Depression in the 1930s.* New York: Clarion Books, 2004.
The author uses eyewitness accounts, archival photos, and stirring text to convey Depression-era pain and suffering. The emphasis is on the "Okies" who fled the dust bowl in a desperate search for jobs in California.

Damon, Duane. *Headin' for Better Times: The Arts of the Great Depression.* Minneapolis: Twenty-First Century Books, 2002.
The Great Depression was not only a time of great struggle but also a time of artistic flowering. This book examines the music, literature, painting, theater, movies, and photography of the era, including the work of such greats as John Steinbeck, Benny Goodman, and Dorothea Lange.

Flynn, Kathryn A. *The New Deal: A 75th Anniversary Celebration.* Layton, UT: Gibbs Smith, Publisher, 2008.
This comprehensive guide to the New Deal features statistics, archival posters, FSA and other photographs, and extensive descriptions of each program, plus recollections from New Deal workers.

Gourley, Catherine. *Rosie and Mrs. America: Perceptions of Women in the 1930s and 1940s.* Minneapolis: Twenty-First Century Books, 2008.
In this award-winning title, Gourley explores women's lives in the 1930s and 1940s. She looks at media images of women (in movies, magazines, and advertisements) and how these images did and more often did not reflect reality.

Litwin, Laura Baskers. *Dorothea Lange: A Life in Pictures.* Berkeley Heights, NJ: Enslow Publishers, 2007.
While working with the Farm Security Administration, Dorothea Lange took pictures of dust bowl migrants and other Americans. Her photograph "Migrant Mother" remains an iconic image of the Great Depression. This book tells her story.

Nelson, Kadir. *We Are the Ship.* New York: Hyperion Books for Children, 2008.
In the 1930s, baseball—like many other U.S. institutions—was segregated. Baseball greats such as Satchel Paige played in the Negro Leagues. This award-winning book explores the history of black baseball.

Sullivan, George. *Knockout! A Photobiography of Boxer Joe Louis.* Des Moines: National Geographic Children's Books, 2008.
Louis was one of the first African American heroes of the twentieth century. When he defeated German boxer Max Schmeling in 1939, his fame soared even higher. This book tells his story with words and pictures.

Viola, Kevin. *Lou Gehrig.* Minneapolis: Twenty-First Century Books, 2005.
The New York Yankees were dominant in baseball throughout the 1930s—largely because of first baseman Lou Gehrig. A powerhouse at the plate, Gehrig set numerous big-league records. This book tells his story—from his boyhood to his tragic death from amyotrophic lateral sclerosis, later called Lou Gehrig's disease.

Films

Amelia Earhart: The Price of Courage. DVD. Newton, NJ: Shanachie Entertainment, 2002.
When Amelia Earhart flew alone across the Atlantic Ocean in 1932, she became a national hero. When her plane disappeared over the Pacific Ocean in 1937, the nation mourned. This film from the acclaimed *American Experience* series tells Earhart's story.

Eleanor Roosevelt. DVD. Hollywood, CA: PBS Paramount, 2006.
Along with her husband, Eleanor Roosevelt helped steer Americans through the dark days of the Depression and World War II. Using interviews, newsreel footage, and other archival material, the filmmakers examine Roosevelt's life and work.

Our Daily Bread and Other Films of the Great Depression. DVD. Chatsworth, CA: Image Entertainment, 1999.
This collection includes both fictional and documentary films created during the 1930s. *Our Daily Bread* is a full-length feature about Americans who start a collective farm to survive the Great Depression. Next, four short documentaries explain New Deal programs. Two more films, which claim to be impartial news features, are actually propaganda films designed to defeat Upton Sinclair in the 1934 California governor's race.

Websites

America in the 1930s
http://xroads.virginia.edu/~1930s/front.html
This elegantly designed website is a gateway to 1930s film, art, and culture. It features vintage advertisements, biographies, a timeline, extensive links, and much more.

Benny Goodman: King of Swing
http://www.bennygoodman.com/
With his clarinet and big band, Goodman had young Americans up on their feet dancing in the late 1930s. From photos to quotes to recordings, this site offers all things Benny Goodman.

Raymond Loewy: The Father of Industrial Design
http://www.raymondloewy.com/
With his streamline product designs, Raymond Loewy gave the 1930s its distinctive, modern look. This website pays homage to the master designer and his work.

SELECTED 1930s CLASSICS

Books

Hammett, Dashiell. *The Thin Man.* 1934. Reprint, New York: Vintage, 1989.
Hammett pioneered the "hard-boiled" detective fiction of the 1930s and 1940s. In *The Thin Man* (later adapted for the movies), amateur sleuths Nick and Nora Charles track a killer.

Hurston, Zora Neale. *Their Eyes Were Watching God.* 1937. Reprint, New York: Harper Perennial, 2006.
Hurston's novel follows the travails of Janie Crawford, a young African American woman. Set in the all-black town of Eaton, Florida, the novel sheds much light on the lives of black Americans in the early twentieth century.

Steinbeck, John. *The Grapes of Wrath.* 1939. Reprint, New York: Penguin, 2002.
Steinbeck tells the wrenching story of the Joad family, who leave the dust bowl-ravished Oklahoma only to find much greater suffering in the migrant camps of California.

Films

Gold Diggers of 1933. DVD. Burbank, CA: Warner Home Video, 2006.
Watch Ginger Rogers, Joan Blondell, Ruby Keeler, and the other showgirls dance their hearts out in this Depression-themed classic. Busby Berkeley's dance numbers are not to be missed.

Gone with the Wind. DVD. Burbank, CA: Warner Home Video, 2006.
Clark Gable plays the dashing Rhett Butler. Vivien Leigh is the fiery Scarlett O'Hara. Based on

Margaret Mitchell's popular novel, this sweeping Civil War epic set box-office records when it premiered in 1939.

Scarface. DVD. Los Angeles, CA: United Artists, 2007.
In the 1920s, gangsters such as Al Capone lorded over vast criminal empires. In the 1930s, Americans flocked to gangster movies, including this 1932 classic starring Paul Muni.

The Wizard of Oz. DVD. Burbank, CA: Warner Brothers Family Entertainment, 1999.
Judy Garland plays Dorothy Gale, a young woman who suddenly lands in the wonderful land of Oz in this 1939 classic. She and her new-found friends seek out the Wizard to help them with their problems, but run into difficulties along the way.

1930s ACTIVITY

Identify six to ten things in your own life or family history that relate to the 1930s. (To get started, consider relatives' or neighbors' lives, family antiques or collections, your house or buildings in your neighborhood, favorite movies, books, songs, and places you've visited.) Use photographs, mementos, and words to create a print or computer scrapbook of your 1930s research.

INDEX

ABOUT THE AUTHORS

Based in California, Edmund Lindop wrote several books for the Presidents Who Dared series as well as several of the titles in The Decades of Twentieth-Century America series.

Margaret J. Goldstein was born in Detroit and graduated from the University of Michigan. She is an editor and author for young readers. She lives in Santa Fe, New Mexico.

PHOTO ACKNOWLEDGMENTS

The images in this book are used with the permission of: © Ralph Morse/Pix Inc./Time & Life Pictures/Getty Images, pp. 3, 113; © Hulton Archive/Getty Images, pp. 4–5, 6–7, 10, 34, 57, 65, 78–79, 94, 97, 106–107, 110, 139 (left, right); © FPG/Hulton Archive/Getty Images, pp. 9, 16, 51; © Dorothea Lange/MPI/Getty Images, pp. 12–13; © John Vachon/Library of Congress/Hulton Archive/Getty Images, pp. 14–15; Library of Congress, pp. 17 (LC-USZ62-24155), 18–19 (LC-USW33-035391-C), 23 (LC-DIG-fsa-8b08252), 25 (LC-DIG-fsa-8b38341), 31 (LC-USZ62-117121), 46 (LC-USZ62-111099) 47 (top) (LC-DIG-npcc-16474), 70 (top left) (LC-USZC2-958), 70 (top right) (LC-USZC2-5191), 70 (bottom left) (LC-USZC2-964), 70 (bottom right) (LC-USZC2-1012), 75 (LC-DIG-van-5a52142), 77 (LC-USF342-008147-A), 86 (LC-USZC2-904), 88 (LC-DIG-fsa-8b29516), 102 (LC-USZC4-2028), 114–115 (LC-DIG-thc-5a47422); © Gabriel Hackett/Hulton Archive/Getty Images, p. 21; AP Photo, pp. 26–27, 30, 43, 48–49, 52, 55, 58–59, 60–61, 66, 68, 80, 83, 92, 93, 100, 101, 103, 104, 105, 109, 112, 116, 117, 119, 120, 121, 122–123, 139 (middle); © American Stock/Getty Images, pp. 28–29, 33; AP Photo/Works Progress Administration, p. 36; © Anthony Potter Collection/Hulton Archive/Getty Images, pp. 38–39; © William Vandivert/Life Magazine/Time & Life Pictures/Getty Images, p. 40; © MPI/Hulton Archive/Getty Images, p. 42; AP Photo/Murray Becker, p. 44; © Topical Press Agency/Hulton Archive/Getty Images, p. 47 (bottom); © Kurt Hutton/Picture Post/Hulton Archive/Getty Images, p. 50; © Popperfoto/Getty Images, p. 53; © Alfred Eisenstaedt/Time & Life Pictures/Getty Images, pp. 62, 85; Courtesy of The State Archives of Florida, p. 64; © Eric Schaal/Time & Life Pictures/Getty Images, p. 72; © Bettmann/CORBIS, pp. 74, 90–91; AP Photo/Frank Filan, p. 81; © Brooklyn Museum/CORBIS, p. 82; *American Gothic*, 1930 by Grant Wood. All rights reserved by the Estate of Nan Wood Graham/Licensed by VAGA, New York, NY. Grant Wood, American, 1891–1942, American Gothic, 1930, Oil on beaver board, 30 11/16 x 25 11/16 in. (78 x 65.3 cm) unframed, Friends of American Art Collection, 1930.934 Photograph by Bob Hashimoto. Reproduction, The Art Institute of Chicago. Photography © The Art Institute of Chicago, p. 84; © Margaret Chute/Hulton Archive/Getty Images, p. 95; SWING TIME © RKO Pictures, Inc. Licensed by Warner Bros. Entertainment Inc. All Rights Reserved. Image provided by © John Kobal Foundation/Hulton Archive/Getty Images, p. 96; KING KONG © RKO Pictures, Inc. Licensed by Warner Bros. Entertainment Inc. All Rights Reserved. Image provided by © Hulton Archive/Getty Images, p. 98; © John Kobal Foundation/Hulton Archive/Getty Images, p. 99; © Charles Peterson/Hulton Archive/Getty Images, p. 108; © Frank Driggs Collection/Hulton Archive/Getty Images, p. 111; © National Baseball Hall of Fame Library/MLB Photos via Getty Images, p. 118; © Heinrich Hoffmann/Timepix/Time & Life Pictures/Getty Images, pp. 124–125; National Archives, pp. 126–127 (W&C 1134); © Monika Graff/The Image Works, p. 128.

Front Cover: Library of Congress (top left) (LC-DIG-fsa-8b29516); © FPG/Hulton Archive/Getty Images (top right); © MPI/Hulton Archive/Getty Images (bottom left); © Keystone/Hulton Archive/Getty Images (bottom right).